What a Master Mason Ought to Know

by
PAPUS

Doctor PAPUS
33°, 90°, 96°

What a
MASTER MASON
Ought to Know

The Rites, the Origin of the Degrees, Legend of HIRAM
Sup. Gr. Marshal of the Sup. Grand Lodge of Manchester (Swed. Rite).
President of the Swedenborgian Grand Lodge of France.
Chapter & Temple INRI
Ven. of the Symb. Lodge Humanidad NQ 240
Director of the Secretariat of the Universal Mas. Federation (Paris).

Translated and Introduced by
Sâr Phosphoros
Sovereign Grand Commander of the
Christian Knights of Saint-Martin

TriadPress
HAINESVILLE, IL

What a Master Mason Ought to Know
by Papus (1910)

Translated and Introduced
by Sâr Phosphoros

First English Edition Published 2022

ISBN: 978-0-9973101-9-1

Triad Press, LLC
260 E. Belvidere Rd. #357
Hainesville, IL 60030

Contents

TRANSLATOR'S INTRODUCTION

This short work, as indicated by its title, is intended not as philosophical treatise on high grade esoteric Masonry, but rather as introduction to some very fundamental concepts that every Blue Lodge Mason should be acquainted with. Now, since our author is the eminent occultist, Papus, these fundamentals are designed, of course, to lead the Mason towards a fuller realization of that Light of which Freemasonry is purported to be the custodian; a Light that ultimately may only be intimately known and made manifest within the purely occult and theurgical grades which could be said to lie outside of Freemasonry proper. But the core or seed of all that is expounded upon in the higher degrees is to be found within the three degrees of Blue Masonry. The grades, known in the Anglo-American Grand Lodge system as Entered Apprentice, Fellowcraft, and Master Mason, are known in the French systems merely as Apprentice, Companion, and Master. The reader who happens to be an initiate of "regular" (a term considered by many to be unfairly prejudicial, and which is treated at length at the end of this volume) American or English Freemasonry will notice some differences in terminology, as well as in the descriptions of some aspects of the degrees. This is due largely to variations that developed as Freemasonry migrated from country to country. In some cases, such as certain degree words, the continental European uses are actually the older versions, the English and American branches having rearranged certain elements after some "secrets" had been exposed. But the purpose of this work is not to try to say that such-and-such Masons are the "right" ones, while "those other guys" have it all wrong. On the contrary, the over-arching theme of this work is Masonic fraternity and universalism.

The era in which this work was composed - or at least compiled, as some of the essays contained herein appear in previous works - was very significant in the realm of occult Freemasonry in Europe. Though published in 1910, the first essay after the introduction was written in 1908, which likely dates the compiling of the majority of the volume. This year of 1908 is of particular interest to us in that it was the year that Papus and his secretary, Victor Blanchard, organized a Masonic and Spiritualist Congress, intended to work towards a sort of universal federation of occult and Masonic rites. This Congress was attended by a number of occult and Masonic luminaries, such as Charles Detre (Téder), René Guénon, Theodor Reuss, Egdardo Frosisi, Henri Durville, Albert Journet, Arnoldo Krumm-Heller, and may others. Among the Masonic rites represented, in addition to various European Grand Lodges, were the Swedenborgian Rite, Le Droit Humain (who hosted the Congress), and the Ancient & Primitive Rite of Memphis-Misraim. Among the para-Masonic and occult orders represented were the Ordo Templi Orientis, the Ordre Kabbalistique de la Rose+Croix, and of course, the Ordre Martiniste.

The grand federation of rites that Papus and Blanchard had hoped for did not materialize at this time, but the Congress was far from a failure. Many important relationships were forged and sealed here that would help shape the future of esoteric Freemasonry and related movements. It was here that Papus would receive a charter for a superior body of Memphis-Misraim in France, as well as that of the OTO. Theodor Reuss received primatial authority from Papus in the Gnostic Church. Dr. Krumm-Heller would receive initiations, ordinations, and empowerments from Papus and others for Martinism, Memphis-Misraim, the Gnostic Church, and other bodies, which he would bring to South America where their descendants thrive to this day. In 1910, the year of this book's publication, according to the official history of the Ordo Templi Orientis Antiqua / La Couleuvre Noire, Papus met with the Haitian, Lucien-François Jean-Main, and conferred upon him the degrees of Martinism and the OTO, and perhaps other rites and degrees. The Haitian movement, said to have had connections with the remnants of the old Élus Cohen Temples of Port-au-Prince and Leogane, as well as to the French and Spanish Gnostic Churches and to the Spanish Memphis-Misraim, would become instrumental in introducing these movements into the United States in the 1960s through Michael Bertiaux, who remains, as of the time of this writing, the head of this particular branch of Memphis-Misraim.

The importance of the Ancient and Primitive Rite of Memphis-Misraim cannot be disregarded. Although it is barely mentioned in this work (which should not really be to surprising, as it concerns principally the Blue degrees), the fact that Papus' name is accompanied by the numbers 33°, 90°, 96° - the degrees represented by the Rite, that is to say the 33° of the Scottish Rite (Cerneau), the 90° of the Rite of Misraim, and the 96° of the Rite of Memphis - shows the importance he attached to it. This Rite of Rites, this compendium of high degrees, has proven to be a useful, if sometimes unwieldy, framework for the very highest of occult instruction. For those wishing to explore this Rite further, in addition to seeking out initiation from one of the bodies extant, we would recommend Tau Palamas' *Spirit Builders: A Free Illuminist Approach to the Antient and Primitive Rite of Memphis+Misraim*.

The sentiments set forth by Papus over a hundred years ago concerning the state of Freemasonry in France are eerily similar to those of American Freemasonry in the present era. Having been active in various Masonic rites for over twenty-five years, including so-called "regular" Freemasonry, where I was raised to the sublime degree degree of Master Mason in 1995, I can say unequivocally that my own observations of the level of ignorance among the "regulars" as concerns the history of

Freemasonry as well as the inner secrets - that is, esoteric interpretations of the degree - was as widespread and thoroughly penetrating as what Papus describes of his own day. This is not to say that there are not true seekers of Light among the mainstream bodies; but they are woefully under-educated by the official channels, sometimes to the point of actively discouraging the pursuit of esoteric wisdom. Thus, this book is for those Masons who are truly seeking more Light. It does not have all the answers, but it may help one to start formulating and asking the right questions. It encourages the Mason to think deeply and freely, leaving behind prejudice, but holding fast to the inner guiding light. Papus shows that Freemasonry is not merely a social organization - though it is that too - but a true gateway to self-discovery, and a stepping stone to the higher mysteries. As a genuine vehicle of the Lesser Mysteries, and portal to the Greater Mysteries, the Blue Lodge should not be disregarded, or its importance underestimated. If you apply the Hermetic axiom, As Above, So Below, which may be better understood as: As Within, So Without, the events and cycles depicted within the Masonic ritual give insight not only to the past, present and future of humanity and Nature, but to the very workings of the human psyche and even those of divinity itself.

In short, these essays, or "pieces of architecture," reveal insights and messages that are just as relevant today as they were in 1910. Indeed, Papus' insights into the human mind and society show a profound level of understanding in their timelessness. Masons of every obedience and even the curious non-initiate cannot help but to find a wealth of information within these brief pages. And if there is one message that should remain with the reader, it is that Freemasonry's best hope of remaining relevant is for its members, "regular" or otherwise, to stay true to its principles of universal brotherhood, tolerance, peace, and unity. Every branch of Freemasonry has an important role to play; and it is upon the Masonic initiates to recognize this fact and exercise not only tolerance, but support for the many, varied, wonderful branches of the Masonic family.

Sâr Phosphoros
S.G.C.
CKSM

INTRODUCTION

We present today to the Masons who desire to study the Masonic Science, a premier collection which is principally intended for the members of the Symbolic Lodges.

It is easy to ascertain that many French Masons are unaware of nearly all of the Masonic Science, and would be quite at a loss to explain why such degree corresponds to such color in the decorations, or to such Hebrew word as a sacred word.

The Masonic Science exists, it is only left to reconstitute many of the secrets of this Venerable Order, and it constitutes an adaptation of the Hebrew Kabbalah on the one hand and of the Gnostic traditions on the other, more or less modified by the Templars.

Without the knowledge of this Masonic Science, it is impossible to seize the marvelous social adaptations placed at the disposal of the E.·. of the T.·. and the means to adapt the Masonic Symbolism to our era and to our new means of teaching and propaganda.

It is easy, after some months of probation in a Lodge, to obtain an increase in wages and to change the color of his decoration; it is more difficult to give a good account of the origins of the symbolic meetings of which he has become an actor, or sometimes a simple figurant.

If Freemasonry is a simple society of social action, why these mysteries, this special language, and these decorations? If all this serves nothing, abolish it without hesitation. But if, under these symbols, hides a high Truth whose knowledge may lead to social adaptations liberating humanity, then let us study this Masonic Science with all the respect which is due to it.

It is not in France, where nearly all the traditions are unfortunately lost, it is with the foreigner: in England, Spain, and especially Germany that I have pursued my research on this point.

In my conversations with the Very Ill. Br. John Yarker, Supreme Chief of the Primitive and Original Rite, with Dr. W. Westcott of the Rosicrucian Society of England, with Villarino del Villar, the illustrious Spanish Mason, and with the Rose-Croix and the Alchemists of Germany, I have been able to study, elsewhere than in some books and in a serious manner, the origin of the Masonic Science.

Many of the foreign Supreme Councils have granted me the great honor of inscribing me among their Honorary Members or to the number of their Representatives in France. I have been all the more touched by this, seeing that I was so violently attacked by certain Frech Masons whose insults I disregard.

One proves the movement in walking. If I have had the chance to penetrate enough into the meaning of the Masonic symbols in order to be in a position to instruct the sincere seeker, my written studies will prove it. If I am only a poor jackdaw in borrowed feathers, my adversaries will be there to demonstrate it. Recall the Arab proverb: the dogs bark, the caravan passes...

I address myself to all those captivated by impartial research, and I tell them:

If the Lodge to which you belong has given you satisfaction, pursue your career there. If, on the contrary, you have not found what you seek there, be discouraged no more. Read this little opuscule and have it read without troubling yourself with its author.

Let us see together whether the passwords and sacred words are not Hebraic words, on which the Kabbalah is alone capable of giving us the true key. Let us study the history of the grades of Écossisme [Scottish Masonry] by surrounding ourselves with all the teachings of the historical critic; let us study the real origins of the diverse Rites which all claim a regularity most problematic for the majority among them.

And above all, let us have no fear of the phantoms. The phantoms are the creation of the Br. Illiterati, chiefs of certain Rites who have a dreadful fear of seeing the BB study in the light of day the... Mysteries... the Secret Traditions!!!!! And all this satisfied their vanity, just as they have not been admitted to the honor of paying an increase in wages.

And we are witness to this ludicrous fact that a Master (let us add "regular" in order to please my adversaries) knew much less about Freemasonry than a Jesuit writer or lecturer on "Christian France." What is very common has no need of any mystery, and the true Masonic Science scoffs at these ridiculous fears.

Let us keep our reason intact, and let us study in the light of day what may instruct us and drive out from our brains all the superstitions; the clerical superstitions as much as the Voltairian superstitions. Let us be free Thinkers, and let us accustom ourselves to analyzing for ourselves the ideas which are presented to us. It will always be the honor of true Masonry to teach its members to distinguish freely the enlightened Science from hateful ignorance. The murderers of Hiram keep watch always at the doors of the Temple, and they always believe themselves more regular than their Architect... Leave them to their said crimes, and the Avengers are not far away.

If the reception of this modest study permits us to pursue our publications, we will arrive successively at the various adaptations of the Masonic Tradition.

Dr. Papus.

THE MASONIC RITES

The Masons may be divided into two categories: the Mason who seeks to be instructed and to understand, and the indifferent Mason.

This last has seen in Freemasonry a means to succeed or to be assisted. For him it is a society like any other, more convenient, that is all.

The Mason who seeks, on the contrary, quickly realizes that there exist teachings which necessitate a cause. He reflects on all that strikes his eyes in the Lodge, from the words that he hears to the ritual that they execute before him, and he discovers then that there must exist a Science of Masonry, as there exists a mathematical science which utilizes algebra.

What, then, are the ideas of the Masonic Science?

If one takes up a position in the domain of history, one realizes that the first centers of elevated Masonic studies have been created in France by the Alchemists, the Mystics, the adepts of the Occult Sciences: Illuminati of Avignon, Rose-Croix, Christian Theosophists, and Martinèsist. They have adapted to Masonry the Secret Science whose tradition they hold.

The Elements of this Science are found:

In the Symbols: symbolic Ciphers and Numbers, Ternary, Quaternary, Septenary, etc.

In the Figures: Triangles, Blazing Star (Pentagram), Seal of Solomon (Hexagram), Tableau of the Lodges.

In the Legends: Legend of Hiram, legend of Solomon, Inri, History of J-B Molay.

In the Tools: Mallet, Level, Rule, Square, Compass, Cubic Stone, Swords, Daggers, etc.

In the Words: Hebrew and Latin Passwords, and Words in the Profane Tongue of the Initiate.

In the Signs: Signs and Touches [Grips] of each degree.

In the Decorations and Jewels: In the Banners.

In the Language written with the secret characters according to the grades.

All this together supposes and necessitates a Particular Science whose study must constitute the initiation into the true Masonry.

It is necessary, however, to remember that Masonry has found itself mixed up with a throng of political events. Understanding the possible usefulness of this admirable association, certain men of the State, or even simple ambitious ones, have wished to utilize this Order in sight of an aim entirely foreign to the social applications of the Masonic Science. From there, the abandon of the symbolic studies and the transformation of Freemasonry into a society of political action, with philosophical teachings with materialist tendencies. The Lodges which follow this path have a strong tendency to abandon symbolic studies which no longer have any usefulness for their members and to disregard the high grades where these studies ought to be pursued.

On the other hand, and this is especially visible to the foreigner, the Masons attached to the ancient formulas have not abandoned the special researches concerning the pure Masonic Science.

It is from these diverse tendencies that are derived the different Masonic systems for the type of instruction, for the work, and even for the ritual initiation.

In Masonic Style, these systems are called Rites, and these Rites may be divided into three principal genres from which the others are derived by fusion or adaptation.

1. The Rites of elementary philosophical studies of immediate political action. They scorn or do not understand all of what comes from this action, and they abandon all study of the pure Masonic Science. The degrees are reduced in number; the trials, physical and otherwise, are abandoned, and the ritual of the high grades ignored. The tendency of these Rites is the transformation of Masonry into a profane society.

The Grand Orient of France or Modern French Rite; some foreign Grand Orients are attached to this system.

2. Aside from these Rites transforming the traditional symbolism, there exist others where the hierarchy and the high grades are scrupulously preserved. The succession of the degrees represents in effect the history of the secret traditions in profane society, from Solomon to the Alchemists, in passing through the Crusaders, the Templars, and all those persecuted by the Papal Egregore. Moreover, the hierarchy of the Teaching in Blue Masonry, Red Masonry, Black Masonry, and White Masonry allows a rational development of the Masonic Science studied successively in the Lodges, in the Chapters, in the Areopagoi, and regularized in its teaching by the General Direction or Supreme Council.

These Rites belong to the Scottish System, which is Scottish only in name, but which is known universally under this appellation.

We cite among the Rites attached to this Scottish system:

The Ancient and Accepted Scottish Rite of Morin, reformed by Pike.

The Ancient and Accepted Scottish Rite of Cerneau.

The Primitive and Original Rite of Freemasonry.

The Spanish National Rite, Ancient and Primitive Rite, the Universal Mixed Rite, etc.

The word "ancient" or "primitive" generally indicates the attachment to the Scottish system, just as the "modern" indicates an attachment to the previous system.

3.   Certain Masons attached to the societies of the Rose-Croix or devoted in a special manner to the study of the Masonic Science, have wished to study this Science thoroughly by adapting Kabbalistic and mystical degrees.

This type of Masonry has always been reserved to an elite, and often includes only high grades, leaving to the other rites the care of preparing the future initiates.

The most known of these Rites is the Rite of Misraim, then the Rite of Memphis, both founded in sight of a special aim. They have often formed Powers united under the name Memphis-Misraim. This Rite has 90 or 96 degrees.

Generally, the members of the foreign Supreme Councils are initiated into the three Rites and are provided with the degrees: 33°, 90°, 96°.

The Swedenborgian Rite and the Orders of Christian Illuminati are attached to these special Rites.

Let one note here that we do only the work of historian. We show the existence and the situation of each genre of Rites, without wishing to judge anything. The impartial seeker ought first of all to state without any rank prejudice, leaving to each intelligent reader the care to conclude in all independence.

Many French Masons are unaware of these fundamental facts of every Masonic organization. They make, moreover, many efforts to hide them from such simple things. In the end, each Rite has the singular pretention of being alone regular. From here, quarrels and excommunications without end. We are now going to speak as clearly as possible on this...

It is evident that each Masonic power, constituted and possessing some Lodges or Chapters, will always look with a very evil eye upon the birth or arrival in its place of action of a new power, or one coming from elsewhere. Immediately forgetting all the teachings of fraternity, tolerance, and truth taught in the official discourses, they go on to conduct themselves with the new creation exactly as a Church conducts itself with a new Church: appeal to the irregularity, major or minor excommunication, forbidding the Brothers from frequenting the new- comers, finally all that they reproach the religious sectarians for.

However, the impartial study of history shows us that a Rite always corresponds to a political or philosophical necessity. It is just as if France was at this moment abandoned by its Masonic directions; it was quickly stricken from the number of countries able to be considered as doing serious Masonic work.

What, then, is the excommunication of a Rite worth in regards to another?

Exactly what the excommunication of a Church is worth in regards to another.

The Reformed are irregular to the Catholics, who themselves as well as the Reformed are irregular to the Orthodox, and all are overwhelmed with historical documents in order to affirm their sole regularity.

Now, it is sad to see men of enlightened reason, who should no longer allow themselves to be influenced by prejudices, to let themselves go to their blinding passions and conduct themselves like the clerical sectarians.

And what is comical in this intrigue, is that those who speak of irregularity are obliged to throw a discreet veil over their own origins, for history is not kind to fabricators of Rituals, and it cruelly returns to their true place the excommunicators of today who were often, if not always, the irregulars of yesterday.

Thus the Grand Orient of France withholds the record of its irregularity. It has been formed by Lacorne and a series of BB expelled from Masonry, for grave reasons. It has been constituted in violation of all the general statutes of Masonry and of all the former and solemn oaths of the constituting BB. Now, as the fallen woman become honest by a marriage towards the end of life, there is no Masonic Power more disposed to speak of the irregularity of the others than the Grand Orient of France and its derivatives like the Swiss Lodge Alpina.

The Ancient and Accepted Scottish Rite of Morin, reformed by Pike, is likewise irregular in its origins, as have demonstrated the BB belonging to the Ancient and Accepted Rite of Cerneau. The Rite of Morin has no regular charter to its origin, and the pretended document of Frederick II is, in the opinion of Albert Pike himself, a sweet pleasantry, not to say a forgery.

Likewise, the Grand Lodge of England, the Power most difficult in matters of Masonic origin, has never been able to produce its patents of constitution, which do not exist.

Ah well! This does not prevent in the least each of the Powers that we just enumerated from possessing in their midst some men of great value from the point of view of the Masonic Science. If we present these historical deductions on regularity, deductions clarified by the scholarly studies of our Br. Teder, it is not to slight any BB of good faith and well instructed. It is in order to show that the Freemasons owe their origin to initiates who have found it good to remain unknown superiors, and who have constituted rites without giving charters, in order to preserve their plan.

In our era when a man makes himself someone without having need of ancestors (*Self Made Man*), it is necessary to have the courage to recognize the men of value in universal Masonry without debating the historical value of each rite from the moment that he initiates the BB into the customary rules, and that he possesses a certain number of Lodges.

There exist, according to the research of the illustrious Br. Villarino del Villar, three hundred thousand Masons attached to the Masonic Powers which are called regular, and two million BB attached to the other Powers.

It seems to us necessary to lay out in all impartiality a picture of all the Masonic Powers without implicating or judging the ones or the others. Then it will be possible to seek a means of unity which respects the autonomy of each rite. It is this way in the United States of America, where the constitution of each State is respected, which does not impede the effective power of the Federation. It is this way in Switzerland. It must be likewise in Freemasonry, where each rite is an autonomous State, however small it is.

Now, a Federation may only be established upon the respect of others.

Freemasonry has always been the great initiator of political and social reforms. It has destroyed for its members the limits and the prejudices of races and colors; it has presided over the destruction of individual titles of nobility and corporative statutes which crush the intelligence of the poor; it has sustained a secular struggle against obscurantism under all its forms.

The moment is come for it to come out of the period of petty quarrels and individual rivalries. The Federation of Rites will precede ;the Federation of the Powers of Europe, and we will respect all the rites, whether they be with us or against us. The work to which we call our BB today requires far too much time and collective efforts for individuals to consider it.

We will all have disappeared from the physical plane long since without doubt, when the FF who will come to gather upon our tombs the branch of acacia and present it to the first federal assembly of the Masonic Powers, while saying: Stand and come to order, my BB, here is the plan of Hiram, which is accomplished. The workers are classed according to their genre of work, and they are going to realize a part of the Great Work of terrestrial humanity.

St. Beatenberg, July 26, 1908.

✝ ⊤ ✚ ✛ ✝ ✠ ⊕ ‡

THE MASONIC DEGREES

Progressive Constitution of the 33 Scottish Degrees

It does not suffice us to know the summary of the history of the different rites. It is necessary for us to penetrate deeper into their knowledge and, all while reserving for a subsequent work a complete and detailed study of the Masonic symbolism, to give to those who are interested in Masonry an idea of the real character of the rites from the point of view of the tradition.

First of all, let us put the readers onward against the studies made by the clericals. We have already spoken on the tendency of these latter to confuse Illuminism and Masonry. Sharing a preconceived idea: the intervention of Satan in the lodges, the writings attached to clericalism have intermingled the analysis of the Masonic rituals with innuendo and the most purely ludicrous personal reflections. Under the appearance of impartial analysis, they slide time and again little commentaries intended to mislead the confident reader. In acting in this way, they remain in their role, that we know personally by experience, and they were worthy of tempting the verve of Leo Taxil, who was mocked by them with such skillfulness, that they have insulted the man; but wholly kept his ideas on the secret role of Occultism in our era.

We are going to analyze the transformations of the ritual by throwing a very general glance upon its historical evolution.

The first Masonic ritual uniting the Masons of the Spirit to those of the same matter, has been composed by illuminated brethren of the Rose-Croix of whom the best known are: Robert Fludd and Elias Ashmole.[1]

KEY OF THE SYMBOLIC GRADES

Apprentice

The first three degrees were established upon the quaternary cycle applied to the denary, that is to say upon the *Hermetic* squaring of the universal circle.

The grade of Apprentice was to uncover, teach, and reveal the first quarter of the circle; the Grade of Companion, the second quarter, and the Grade of Master the last two quarters and the center.

The significance attributed by the revealer to each degree derives directly from the total significance of the circle and its particular adaptation.

Thus, if the adaptation of the circle is related to the movement of the earth upon itself, the first quarter of the circle will symbolically describe the coming out from the night, from six o'clock in the morning until nine o'clock; the second quarter of the circle, the ascension from nine o'clock to noon; and the last two quarters, the descent towards night, or noon of the evening.

In this case, the Apprentice will be the man of the morning, and of the rising sun; the Companion, the man of noon or of the full sun; and the Master, the man of the setting sun.

If the adaptation of the circle is related to the (apparent) march of the Sun in the year, the quarters of the circle will correspond to the seasons and represent respectively the Spring, Summer, Autumn, and Winter.

The Apprentice will then be the seed which opens; the Companion the plant which flowers; the Master, the plant which fructifies, and the fruit falls in order to generate new plants by the fructification which frees the seeds contained in it.

Each of these adaptations being able to be applied to the physical world, to the mental world, or to the spiritual world, we may understand how true illuminati may really lead towards the light of truth, towards that "light which illumines every man coming into the world," towards the divine living Word, the profanes called to initiation.

But for this, it would be necessary that, the fundamental and Hermetic key of the degrees and their adaptation was preserved by an occult university. Such was the role that has been reserved to the Rose-Croix and the Judea-Christian initiates. They always have these keys of which the purely Masonic writers have seen only the adaptations; and the present work, though very summarized, will open to this subject the eyes of those who have eyes to see and ears to hear. Let the others insult us and accuse us of worshipping the devil, or of serving the Jesuits; we will let them talk and shrug our shoulders.

From the alchemical point of view, the first three degrees

represented the preparation of the work: the works of the Apprentice representing the material works, those of the Companion representing the research of the true philosophical fire, and the degree of Master corresponding to the putting of the philosophical mercury into the athanor and to the production of the color black, from where
is to come the brilliant colors.

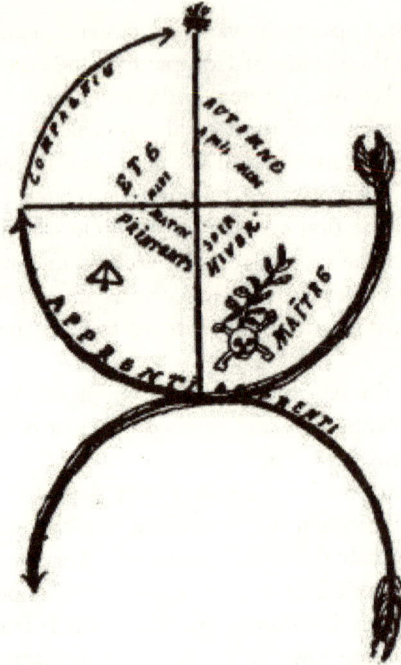

It is truly necessary to have no realization of the ideas and works of the Rose-Croix Hermeticists, in order not to see that true occultists will establish their initiatic framework according to the strict rules of the adaptation of the principles, and that the vengeance of an ousted pretender will play only a very secondary rule in the affair.

Coming from the circle of the profane world, the Apprentice will return there much later in the state of Master, after having acquired initiation. Thus is figured the Hermetic caduceus which gives the real key to the symbolic degrees.

Martinès knew it, as every illuminati, since he has devised his initiation by the *quarter circle*.

One cannot pass from one plane to another but in traversing the kingdom of obscurity and death; such is the first teaching that is indicated to the future initiate by the chamber of reflection and its symbols.

The initiate cannot ever begin alone, under pain of grave accidents; he must, therefore, be assured by visible guides having already acquired the experience, such is the teaching which is extricated from the discourses and the interrogations in which the future Apprentice will take part, upon his entrance into the Lodge.

But the oral teachings would not have any value without the personal experience, such is the aim *of the travels and of the trials* of the different degrees.

Companion

The Apprentice believes without changing plane. He passes from material works to the works concerning the astral forces. He learns to handle the instruments which allow the transformation of matter under the effect of physical forces wielded by the intelligence; he learns also that outside of the physical forces exist forces of a more elevated order, represented by the blazing of the star: these are the astral forces that they let him have a presentiment of without naming them, by virtue of the blazing star.

The Apprentice becomes in this way Companion, and he is instructed on the elements of the *history* of the tradition.

Master

The Companion who is going to become Master must prepare himself to change planes. He will then pass anew into the kingdom of obscurity and death; but, this time, he will pass there alone and without having need of guide. He will do *consciously* what he had done unconsciously in the chamber of reflection.

But, formerly, he received the key of the three degrees and their relationships, contained within the history of *Hiram* and his three murderers.

Just as we have previously demonstrated[2], the solar adaptation of the legend is only an adaptation of a much more general principle: the circulation of the circle in the quaternary, with its two phases of evolution and involution.

But what must be retained for the moment, is that the initiate is not only going to hear this legend, *he is going to live it* in becoming the principal personage of its reproduction.

Here appeared a most remarkable process put into practice by Ashmole, who composed this grade in 1649 (those of Apprentice and Companion had been composed respectively in 1646 and 1648). In order to teach the initiate the history of the tradition in a truly useful manner, they are going to make him relive it. Such will be the key of the subsequent degrees and their ritual. Such is the authentication that it is necessary to always have present in one's mind when it is a question of reforming the rituals in adapting them to new eras, without taking away from their principle of constitution.

CONTRIBUTION OF THE TEMPLAR DEGREES

Ramsay

In order to avoid any obscurity or any fastidious enumeration, let us follow the evolution of the Masonic degrees.

To the three purely symbolic degrees of Apprentice, Companion, and Master, Ramsay adds, in 1738, three new degrees called Ecossais [Scottish], *Novice*, and *Knight of the Temple*.

These grades are *exclusively Templar* and have as their aim to have relived in the new member:

1. The birth and constitution of the Order of the Temple, which continues the Temple of Solomon.

2. The exterior destruction and the secret preservation of the Order.

3. To reap vengeance on the authors of the destruction.

Such is the key of the three grades, which have been adapted to the legend of Hiram, thus attaching the Temple of Jerusalem to the Order of Jacobus Burgundus Molay.

The Masons who wanted to conquer the superior degrees were to be instructed in Occultism and the first elements of the Kabbalah. Thus, the Novice (becoming Royal Arch much later) learned the divine names that are here:

Iod (Principium)	י
Iao (Existens)	יהו
Iah (Deus)	יה
Eheieh (Sum, ero)	אהיה
Eliah (Fortis)	אליה
Iahib (Concedens)	יהב
Adonai (Domini)	אדני
Elchanan (Misericors Deus)	אלחנן
Iobel (Jubilans)	יובל

They have him, at the same time, study the relationships of the letters and the numbers, and the first elements of the symbolism of the forms.

In the following grade, *Écossais* [Scottish] (become Grand Ecossais much later), they joined, to these first studies, others more profound on the correspondences in nature. It is thus that the following table of correspondences of the Stones of the Rational and the divine names indicated the first elements of these studies.

Stones of the Rational	Divine Name Engraved	Significance
Sardonyx	Melek	*Rex*
Topaz	Gomel	*Retribuens*
Emerald	Adar	*Magnificus*
Carbuncle	Ioah	*Deus fortis*
Sapphire	Hain	*Fons*
Diamond	Elchai	*Deus Vivens*
Syncure	Elohim	*Dii* (Sin, the Gods)
Agate	El	*Fortis*
Amethyst	Iaoh	IAΩ
Chrysolite	Ischliob	*Pater excelsus*
Onyx	Adonai	*Domini*
Beryl	IHVH	*(Sum qui sum)*

The initiation into these two degrees developed the union between the Temple of Solomon and the Templars, and it was done in subterranean places in order to expose the necessity to which the Order had been reduced.

It is in the grade of *Knight of the Temple* (become, in part, Kadosh) that the new member was truly consecrated living avenger of the Order. Thus, they transformed the initiation into a political war with which the Martinists have always refused to be associated.

The following words, engraved upon the tomb of Molay, indicated, furthermore, that the processes extending unto the threshold of the second death were known to those who constituted this grade.

Whoever will be able to conquer the terrors of death will come out of the bosom of the earth and will have the right to be initiated into the greater mysteries.

The detail of the initiation of Kadosh with its four chambers, the Black where presides the Grand Master of the Templars, the White where reigns Zoroaster, the Blue where rules the chief of the Tribunal of *Sainte-Wœhme*, and the Red where Frederick directs the works, indicates that this grade is the summary of all the vengeances, and the materialization upon the earth of this terrible book of blood, which is opened too often in the invisible when God allows the inferiors to manifest themselves.

It is this degree which has always been condemned by the Martinists, who prefer prayer to political vengeance, and who want to be the loyal soldiers of the One who said: *"Who strikes by the sword, shall perish by the sword."*

∴

The Templar Rite included, not only these four degrees of Ramsay, but indeed eight degrees that the M. Rosen in his *Satan démasqué* (with whom must have collaborated some good clerical, for the author is too educated to have said all the naiveties contained in this work) attached wrongly, in our opinion, to the Scottish degrees from the 19th to the 28th.

Degrees of the Templar Rite

1° Apprentice or Initiate;
2° Companion or Initiate of the Interior;
3° Adept;
4° Adept of the East [Orient]
5° Adept of the Black Eagle of Saint John;
6° Perfect Adept of the Pelican;
7° Squire;
8° Knight Guardian of the Inner Tower.

THE RITE OF PERFECTION

Analysis of its Degrees

It is to these Templar grades that the constitution of the Rite of Perfection (1758) came to add the complement of the entire Masonic system thus constituted:

1. An historical and moral section in which the candidate relives the history of the first Temple of Jerusalem, from tis construction until its destruction; then he participates in the discovery of the Word which, in becoming incarnate, is going to give birth to Christianity and to the New Jerusalem, of which the candidate become a knight.

Analogically, this historical section allowed profound moral dissertations on the fall and natural reintegration of the human being.

2. An Hermetic section, dedicated to the development of the hyperphysical faculties of the human being, to the initiatic ceremonies, reproduced the phases of the astral splitting and of the alchemical adaptations.

3. To these two sections was added, as we have said, the Templar section.

Let us rapidly analyze the 25 degrees of the Rite of Perfection in order to better clarify the previous classification.

From the 4th to the 15th degree, the president of the lodge represents either Solomon or one of his aides or vassals. One is occupied with either the construction of the Temple or with the vengeance of Hiram or his replacement.

It is this idea of vengeance which has made Rosen[3] believe that the grades of the Élu were related to the *Sainte-Wœhme*. This is an error that an illuminati would not have been able to commit. The *Sainte-Wœhme* has been a Germanic adaptation of the Pythagorean avengers, themselves imitators of the avengers of Osiris, as the author of *Thuileur de l'Ecossisme* has very well seen, and yet Aulnaye has not gone beyond the lesser mysteries and has only understood in the initiation the naturalist side and the sexual plan, as the clericals do today. The following extract will enlighten us on the subject:

"If the third degree of Masonry, that of Master, offers us the picture of the death of Hiram, called the *Architect of the Temple*, or rather of that of Osiris, of Pan, of Tammuz, Grand Architect of Nature, with the first elect is escaped the first cry of vengeance, that which Horus carried out against the murderers of his father, Jupiter against Saturn, etc. This great and permanent system of vengeance, which is found more or less clearly expressed in a multitude of degrees, and notably in the Kadosh, goes back to the most distant times. Independently of the interpretation that one may find of it in the very operations of Nature which present a series of combats and reactions, between the principal generator and the principal destroyer, it belongs especially to theocracy, the most ancient of governments. According to the different circumstances where the founders of the secret societies have found themselves, and according to the particular spirit which animates them, they have made the application of this vengeance to such or such legend, to such or such historical fact; from there, the different rites; but the fundamental principles are always the same."[4]

At the 17th degree (Knight of the East and West), we arrive at the taking of Jerusalem by the Romans and the destruction of the Temple.

It is then that we find the truly Christian degree of Masonry, that degree to which the Rose-Croix have given the name of their Order, and in which they have contained the purest part of the tradition. Thus the materialists, not understanding anything therein, will say that this degree is a creation of the Jesuits; and the Jesuits, moved to see the cross and the glorious Christ in a Masonic Temple, will say that this degree is a creation of Satan.

As they see it, there are degrees for all tastes.

The degree of Masonic Rose-Croix is the physical translation of the mysteries which lead to the title of Illuminated Brother of the Rose-Croix, title not belonging to Freemasonry, but to its creator: the Society of the Illuminati. A Rose-Croix Mason, when he knows his grade well, may be considered as an Apprentice Illuminati, and he possesses all the elements of a high spiritual development, as we are going to see by analyzing this degree.

THE MASONIC ROSE-CROIX

The initiation into the degree of Masonic Rose-Croix requires four chambers: the Green, the Black, the Astral, and the Red, which they generally reduce, in practice, to three by suppressing the first.

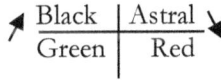

$$\nearrow \quad \frac{\text{Black} \mid \text{Astral}}{\text{Green} \mid \text{Red}} \quad \searrow$$

The theme of the grade is that the Word which is to allow the reconstruction of the Temple has been lost. The candidate finds it, it is the name of O. L. Jesus Christ: INRI, and, thanks to the word, he traverses the astral region in its inferior or infernal section, and he makes his way into the chamber of Christian purification and reintegration.

From the alchemical point of view, it is the creation of the red stone through the discovery of the astral forces, the coming out of the crow's head and the passage to the phoenix or pelican.

From the moral point of view, it is the birth in man of the spark of the divine Word, contained within his soul, by the exercise of prayer, charity, sacrifice, and submission to Christ.

Go, then, to make this understood by a wine merchant, electioneering agent, and dignitary of the Grand Orient, or by an R. -P. Jesuit. The first will replace Faith, Hope, and Charity with his beloved motto Liberty, Equality, Fraternity... or Death, and the second will absolutely want to find anagrams which transform the name of Christ into that of the Prince of the World, for he cannot conceive that one may understand Christ without passing through the costly intermediary of those who think themselves to be the sole divine clergy upon the earth. For the clerical, it is all "Gnosticism"; and he means by this word all that he doesn't understand.

Let us return to the analysis of the initiation.

The green chamber recalls the first evolution of the candidate in the symbolic degrees.

The black chamber is going to open to him the doors of the second death. It is going to indicate a change of plane. It is hung in black, with silver teardrops.

The destruction of the first Temple is represented by the broken columns and instruments of construction strewn on the ground. Three columns remain alone standing, and the transparency which rises above them reads: FAITH, in the SW; HOPE, in the SE; and CHARITY, in the NW.

At the east is one of the most profound symbols, first of all a table, covered by a black cloth, and upon which is found, beyond the instruments of material construction (compass, square, triangle) the symbol of the creation by man of his spiritual being: the Cross bearing a rose at the intersection of each of its arms.

This table is placed before a large curtain which, in being separated, will allow one to see Christ crucified, lighted by two wax candles of solar color.

∴

It is here that the candidate will find the "lost Word," after having first re-created within him *Faith* based on personal work; then *Charity*, which opens to him the doors, very large, of *Hope*, of *Immortality*.

This immortality, he is going to immediately acquire the symbolic certitude of it, for, the face re-covered by a black veil, he penetrates, *aided by those who have passed before him*, into the chamber that we call astral and that they generally call infernal.

Let us say to this purpose, and in order to please M. Antonini[5] that what the Catholics call Hell is called by the occultists the "inferior astral plane." In order to reach heaven, it is necessary to traverse the astral plane and triumph, by his moral purity and by his spiritual elevation, over the larvae and beings which populate this region of the Invisible. Heaven sends to its elect guides in order to pass across this region, and the author of the *Pistis Sophia* gives interesting teachings on this subject. But the occultists put the larvae and the demons in their true place and they do not worship them, reserving their prayers for Christ or the Virgin. It is necessary to triumph over the demons in order to reach the celestial plane; and one only triumphs over them by following the evangelical precepts, in the Occident, or in following the revelations of the masters, in the Orient. Every man of good, be he Christian, Muslim, or Buddhist, is going to heaven when he has followed the word of God; and every criminal, be he pope, Catholic priest, Jew, Protestant, or simple laity of no matter what religion, is going to make the acquaintance of the beings of the astral plane, until the dissolution of his shells, unless divine mercy erases the imprint of his faults. That is why Dante saw several popes in hell.

This astral chamber is formed by a transparency at each end of which is a skeleton, to indicate well that death is the sole door to enter or come out of this chamber. On the transparency, they have painted larvae and whatever astral beings, that the candidate sees while lifting up the veil which covers his head.

He arrives thus at the red chamber, lighted by 33 lights.

At the Orient, under a canopy, the candidate sees an admirable symbol. Above a blazing star bearing the letter ש (shin) reversed in order to indicated the incarnation of the divine Word into human nature. Below is an open and empty sepulcher to show that Christ has triumphed over death, thus indicating the path to all those who would follow him.

Also in this direction is the standard of the chapter upon which is engraved the Pelican, standing over its nest and nourishing its seven little ones with its blood that it makes flow by piercing its own side with its beak. This Pelican bears upon its chest the Rose-Croix. Such is the symbol of the true Knight of Christ; such is the representation of incessant action of the divine light which gives life to even those who commit atrocities in its name, as the sun enlightens the good and the wicked spread over the seven planetary regions of its system.

The inscriptions of the columns: Infinity and Immortality, characterize the spiritual transformation of the virtues illuminating the black chamber.

This initiation is supported by fifteen points of instruction which successively transform the candidate into a Knight of Heredom, Knight Guardian of the Tower of the Rose-Croix. These instructions bear upon the following points:

1st, Mastery; 2nd, the numbers 9, 7, 5, and 3; 3rd, the angular stone; 4th, the mystery of the arch and of immortality (Enoch and Elijah); 5th, the mountains of salvation, Moriah and Calvary, in all the planes; 6th, the Hermetic athanor; 7th, the moral virtues born from spiritual effort; 8th, the resistance to the passions (Guardian of the Tower); 9th, the astral symbolism; 10th, the general symbolism; 11th, the numeric symbolism; 12th, the Christian Jerusalem and the new universal Temple; 13th, the three Christian lights: Jesus, Mary, Joseph; 14th, the lost word; 15th, Consummatum est.

Finally, the Illuminati had transmitted to Masonry, in this degree, their system of Kabbalistic reduction of the names in their consonants and the five points representing the apprenticeship of Illuminism.

.˙.

The following degrees: 19, Grand Pontiff; 20, Grand Patriarch; 21, Grand Master of the Key; 22, Prince of Liban, continue to put into action the historical tradition.

This last grade, Prince of Lebanon, has become the Knight Royal Axe of Scottish Masonry, and it begins the series of true Hermetic degrees dedicated to the development of spiritual faculties.

The initiatic theme of these Hermetic grades bears upon the part of his life when Solomon had given himself to the study of magic and alchemy. One thus sees Solomon submitting to the trials of the second death, of the abandon of the true God for the idols, and returning to the true faith by science. This is a return to another plane of historical allegory of the preceding degrees.

In the Masonry of Perfection, the Hermetic grades were contained in the following degrees: 22, Prince of Lebanon; 23, Prince Adept; and 25, Prince of the Royal Secret.

We rediscover in this degree of Prince Adept, become the 28° of the Scottish Rite, Knight of the Sun, these serious theoretical studies which form the basis of all real practice.

It is with respect to Scottish Masonry, and because of the developments that it has given to these Hermetic grades, that we will study this section in detail.

As one sees, the Rite of Perfection contained the whole Masonic system and the transformations that it will have undergone will bear only upon the developments of degrees already existing in the "Council of Emperors of the East and West."

Let us move on, then, to Scottish Masonry; but first, let us enumerate the seven classes comprising the degrees of this Rite:

1st Class - 1, 2, 3.
2nd Class – 4, 5, 6, 7, and 8.
3rd Class – 9, 10, 11.
4th Class - 12, 13, 14.
5th Class - 15, 16, 17, 18, 19.
6th Class - 20, 21, 22.
7th Class - 23, 24, 25.

SCOTTISH MASONRY
Raison d'être of its New Degrees
Illuminism, Reintegration, and Hermeticism

We come to Scottish Masonry proper, that is to say to the development of the final degrees of the Rite of Perfection.

As we just said, the mysteries of the conscious dividing in two of the human being that they have called the *conscious leaving of the astral body* and which characterized the *baptism* in the ancient temples, these mysteries have been developed in order to constitute the Scottish degrees, added by the Supreme Council of Charleston, in 1802, to the system brought by Morin.

It is not just, therefore, to see in these grades but useless superfluity. They end the progression of the development of the human being by giving him the key to use supra-human faculties, at least in the present life. We say the key, for an initiation cannot give anything else.

What does it matter, after this, that these lights be given to men who see therein only a ridiculous symbolism, or that they blind clericals who seek therein the phallus and kteis, according to their laudable custom;

for they have a brain made thus that they see only this everywhere, with some devil for conductor - Poor folks!

The initiation is going to retrace the various phases of the conscious passage of the astral planes, with its dangers, its perils, and its crowning which is to overcome the circle of the astral hell in order to be raised, if the soul is worthy, into the various celestial regions.

The theme will represent, as we have said, the candidate under the figure of occultist Solomon directing Hiram, in taking part personally in the operations.

The 22°, *Knight Royal Axe*, is related to the *material* preparations of the operations represented by the cutting of the cedars on the Lebanon mountain and by the consecrated axe.

The 23°, Key of the Tabernacle, is related to the indications concerning the plane in which one is going to operate, that is to say the astral nature. The room is perfectly round, lighted by seven principal luminaries and 49=13 (figure of the passage into the astral) accessory lights. The sacred word is IHVH and the password is the name of the Angel of Fire who is to come to assist the operators who, in order to go more quickly, call out to the inferior forces of the astral and risk losing communication with heaven, in allowing himself to be deceived by the demon, represented here by the idols to which Solomon sacrificed. The candidate must come out triumphant from this first contact with the astral region.

It is then that he arrives at the plane where are engraved the *astral impressions*. He sees the word of God, that of the twelve commandments, and that of the Gospels written upon the eternal book, and he then accomplishes the first *travel in God* (password, 24°).

It is there that he awaits the plane of ecstasy where is found Moses when he was illuminated by the burning bush. He just passed the astral plane, he arrives at the divine plane and he has the first manifestation of the celestial harmony (25°). The candidate has as a sign that of the cross, and the sacred word is Moses, the password is Inri, in order to indicate the union of the two Testaments. The chains which surround the candidate indicate the weight of matter and of the shell which paralyzes the action of the Spirit in the divine plane, and the bronze serpent, coiled around the cross, indicates the domination of the astral plane (the serpent) by the man regenerated by Christ (the cross).

The clericals have not been able, to their great regret, to find any devil in this degree. Thus, they generally pass it in silence.

Pursuing his evolution in the invisible plane, the candidate arrives at the various planes of the celestial region (26°, Scottish Trinitarian or Prince of Mercy). He is going to pass through the first, second, and third heaven, and instead of the demons of the astral plane, he is going to make contact with the sylphs and the celestial receivers.

Thus is it necessary to see the ironic chucklings of the ignorant when they occupy themselves with this degree, and the joyous comentaries of the clericals. But let us proceed:

The candidate receives *wings* as mark of his ascension unto the divine plane.

The catechism contains these characteristic phrases:

Q. Are you a Scottish Trinitarian Master?

A. I have seen the *Great Light* and am, like you, *Very Excellent*, by the *triple covenant* of the blood of Jesus Christ, of which you and I bear the mark.

Q. What is this triple covenant?

A. The one that the Eternal made with Abraham by the circumcision; the one that he made with his people in the desert, through the undertakings of Moses; and the one that he made with men through the death and passion of Jesus Christ, his son.

In the following degree (27th), Grand Commander of the Temple, the candidate is admitted into the *Celestial Court* and the jewel bears in Hebraic letters ׳ ר נ ׳, that is to say INRI. The sign consists in forming a cross on the forehead of the brother who questions.

We arrive, thus at the grade which originally contained all the preceding ones, the degree of *Knight of the Sun* (28°), the old Prince Adept of the Rite of Perfection.

This degree symbolizes the reintegration of the Spirit into Adam Kadmon, when he has been judged worthy by God. The candidate finds himself transported into the intra-zodiacal space where man was before the fall, and he notices seven planetary Angels who preside, since the fall, over the destinies of the seven regions, for the candidate is supposed to find himself in the sun. He is going to begin to notice forces emanated from this center. Here are the correspondences first taught in this grade, whose password, purely alchemical, is *Stibium*:

Michael	*Pauper Dei*	Saturn
Gabriel	*Fortitudo Dei*	Jupiter
Ouriel	*Ignis Dei*	Mars
Zerachiel	*Oriens Deus*	Sun
Chamaliel	*Indulgentia Dei*	Venus
Raphael	*Medicina Dei*	Mercury
Tsaphiel	*Absconditus Deus*	Moon

The 29th grade (Grand Scot of Saint Andrew) is essentially alchemical. The adept is supposed to be returned upon the earth after his ascension into the world of principles, and capable of realizing the Great

Work.

To this degree they have added, as sacred word, a cry of vengeance, which shows that they have mixed some points of the Templar Rite with the Hermetic teachings. Here are the passwords of this degree, which are clear enough on this subject:

PASSWORDS OF THE 29°
Ardarel.... Angel of Fire
Casmaran.... Angel of Air
Talliud.... Angel of Water
Furlac.... Angel of Earth

∴

Among the administrative grades: 31°, 32°, 33°, we point out especially the 32°, the old 25° of the Rite of Perfection: *Prince of the Royal Secret.*

The false Frederick of this grade must be left aside, as well as that of the 21° (Noachite); it is a simply historical reconstitution of the Sainte-Wœhme.

What interests us is the figure of this degree, the "seal" where we see five rays of light surrounding a circle and themselves inscribed in another circle, enclosed in a triangle, around which is a pentagon, which reproduced the analysis of the Sphinx, Bull, Lion, Eagle (with two heads) and flaming winged heart, all dominated by a cubic stone. Around the seal are the encampments representing the centers of Masonic realization.

The 33° is, in part, the alchemical development of the Prince of the Royal Secret, and in part a composition to the false Frederick, which does not interest us. It constitutes the administrative grade of the Masonic centers which may be attached to some illuminism.

General summary and recapitulation of the Masonic Degrees

The glance that we have just thrown upon the hierarchy of the Masonic degrees shows us that they constitute a real harmonic progression, in which are encountered scarcely any anomalies, like the Noachite degrees, composed outside of the action of the founders of the Masonic system.

The symbolic degrees contain indeed *in germ* the whole system, but the high grades harmonically develop this germ, first under the historical point of view, inspecting the Jewish people, then Christianity, then the secret Tribunal, the Orders of chivalry and the Templars.

This system would be incomplete without the truly occult crowning, opening to the initiate new views on the salvation of the human

Being by prayer, devotion (18°) and charity which lead to the trials of the second death and to the perception of the divine plane after having triumphed over the infernal temptations of the astral plane. The Illuminati have therefore personally given to their work all its developments; as they will know how to recreate it if it ends up in base materialism and atheism.

The following table will summarize the general meaning of the different degrees.

Symbolic Degrees 1°, 2°, & 3°	Synthetic history of man

Historical Degrees 4° to 22°	Construction of the Temple of Jerusalem Captivity Deliverance Fall of Jerusalem and destruction of the Temple Christianity (18°) New Jerusalem

Templar Degrees 21°, 13°, 14°, and 30°	Secret Tribunal Knights and Templars

Hermetic Degrees 22° to 33°	First trials of the Adept The Adept makes contact with the Astral Serpent Dividing in two The Adept triumphs over the Astral Serpent and rises to the Divine Plane The Hermetic Triumph Reintegration and conscious return to the physical plane.

The progressive evolution of the degrees appear to us then in the following manner (see the table hereafter):

1. Three symbolic degrees.
2. Three Templar high grades of Ramsay, which are to be placed facing nos. 13, 14, and 30.
3. Constitution of the historical degrees, development of the history of Solomon and the construction of the Temple of Jerusalem, 4 to 15; destruction of the Temple and reconstitution of the New Jerusalem by Christianity, 15 to 22.

4. Crowning of the historical grades by the degrees of Hermeticism, opening a door to Christian Illuminism, 22 to 25.

Such is the summary of the Rite of Perfection.

To the twenty-five degrees of the Rite of Perfection the Supreme Council of Charleston has brought the following changes:

Several new degrees were added, they are: Chief of the Tabernacle (23), Prince of Mercy (24), Knight of the Brazen Serpent (25), and Commander of the Temple (26), Knight of the Sun (27). The Prince of the Royal Secret occupied the degrees of 28, 29, 30, and 32; the Kadosh, the 28th degree; and Sovereign Grand Inspector General, the 33rd and last.

At the arrival of de Grasse Tilly at Paris, a new disposition was adopted which governed Scottish Masonry. Here it is in its main lines: (24°) Prince of Mercy became Prince of the Tabernacle; the Commander of the Temple became Scottish Trinitarian (26°); Knight of the Sun becomes the 28th degree and was replaced by the Grand Commander of the Temple; the 29th degree was the Grand Scot of Saint Andrew, and the Kadosh (old 24° of the Rite of Perfection and 28° of Charleston) definitively became the 30°.

The 31° was the Grand Inspector; the Prince Adept constituted the 32°, and the Sovereign Grand Inspector General the 33rd and last degree. Finally, a degree of Noachite, the 21°, replaced everywhere the Grand Master of the Key of the Rite of Perfection.

	(Rite of Perfection)	*(Supreme Council of Charleston)*	*(Convent of Lausanne)*
1. Apprentice			"
2. Companion	"		"
3. Master	"	"	"
4. "	Secret Master	"	"
5. "	Perfect Master	"	"
6. "	Intimate Secretary	"	"
7. "	Provost and Judge	"	"
8. "	Intendant of the Building	"	"
9. "	Élu of the Nine	"	"
10. "	Élu of the Fifteen	"	"
11. p -	Illustrious Élu	"	"
12. *(Ramsay)*	Grand Master Architect	"	"
13. – Écossais	Royal Arch of Enoch	"	"
14. – Novice	Grand Elect, old Perfect Master	"	"
15. "	Knight of the Sword	Knight of the East	"

16. "	Prince of Jerusalem	"	"
17. "	Knight of the East and West	"	"
18. "	Knight Rose-Croix	"	"
19. "	Grand Pontiff	"	"
20. "	Grand Patriarch	Grand Master of all Lodges	Venerable Grand Master of Lodges
21. "	Grand Master of the Key	Noachite Patriarch	Noachite
22. "	Prince of Lebanon	Royal Axe or Prince of Lebanon	Knight Royal Axe
23. "	"	Chief of the Tabernacle	Chief of the Tabernacle
24. "	"	Prince of Mercy	Prince of the Tabernacle
25. "	"	Knight of the Brazen Serpent	Knight of the Brazen Serpent
26. "	"	Commander of the Temple	Scottish Trinitarian
27. "	"	Knight of the Sun	Grand Commander of the Temple
28. "	Prince Adept (23)	Kadosh	Knight of the Sun
29. "	"	"	Grand Scot of Saint Andrew
30. Knight of the Temple	Knight Commander of the Black & White Eagle (24)	Prince of the Royal Secret	Kadosh
31. "	"	Sovereign Grand Inspector General	Grand Inspector
32. "	Sovereign Prince of Masonry, Sublime Comm. of the Royal Secret (25)	"	Sublime Prince of the Royal Secret
33. "	"	"	Sovereign Grand Inspector General

ON THE SYMBOLS AND THEIR TRANSLATION

A word on the subject of the translation of the symbols, in all their adaptations.

A symbol is a material image of a principle, to which it is attached allegorically. Therefore, the symbol expresses the entire analogical ladder of correspondences of its class, from the most elevated to the most inferior.

It is thus that a coarse sectarian may say that the flag is only a painted broomstick, supporting three colored rags. In this case he materializes, in order to disparage it, the idea so beautiful and so pure of the symbolic representation of the Fatherland.

Thus this process of denigration consisting of giving to the symbols their most trivial analogical correspondence will be employed with ravishment by the clerical writers analyzing the Masonic symbols.

The active creative principle and the passive generative principle, symbolized in the Catholic Church by the action of the Father and the Son, have, as inferior sexual correspondence, the phallus and the kteis. So the clericals have not failed to recount to their readers that all the Masonic symbolism, or the whole initiatic tradition of the Illuminati, was reduced to representations of these organs. This is by ignorance or bad faith, and it is only necessary to shrug the shoulders before such behavior.

What would the clericals say, if one turned their method back upon them by showing them that in reasoning with their mentality one may say that the aspergillum is an image of the fertilizing phallus, and that the holy water represents, in this case, the emission of the generative substance; that it is the same of the cross of the bishop, whereas the chalices are kteic representations! What, then, would men actually educated say of these coarse and improper analogies? They would say that it is proof of a singular state of mind, quite bordering on senility.

Thus it seems to us that it is a service to render to the Catholic writers to pray them to study a little better what is meant by a ladder of analogical correspondences, and to not consider the symbols, even Masonic ones, in this coarse light; for they risk seeing this in their own as well, and this is not spiritual and true, either on one side or the other.[6] Here are some notes on the symbolism of the colors employed by the hangings, then on the sacred word that we borrow from l'Aunaye.

The white is consecrated to the *Divinity*; the black, to Hiram and to Christ[7]; thus it is found in the Master, the *Élu*, the *Kadosh*, and in the *Rose-Croix*. The green, emblem of *Life and Hope*, is also that of Zerubbabel; that is why it is the color of the *Perfect Master* and of the *Knight of the East*. The red belongs to Moses, and especially to Abraham; by this right, it is the special color of the *Scottish* system. Finally, the blue, which, as symbol of the celestial abode, is the color of the Sublime Écossais, refers, among the Patriarchs, to Adam, created in innocence in the image of God, and residing in the garden of Eden.[8]

A symbol of the *primitive Word*, the Jehovah belongs specially to the *Ancient Master* or *Perfect Master*, and as *rediscovered Word* to the true Scottish Mason, consecrator of the priest of Jehovah, or of the old law, as opposed to the new. It is found particularly in the Royal Arch, in the Écossais of Perfection, in the Master *ad Vitam*, the Perfect Élu, the Supreme Élu, the Écossais of Prussia, of Montpellier, the Interior of the Temple, etc.[9]

THE CRY OF ALARM

It is following a capital error that French Freemasonry, pushed without its knowledge by foreign agents, has let itself be caught up in political battles. They have shown it the specter of clericalism as one shows the red cape to the bull. They have exalted the materialist tendencies of its members under the pretext of making "free spirits" of them and men of reason"; and from anticlericalism to atheism there was but one step that these simple-minded have soon cleared. To what use was it to speak of this "Great Architect of the Universe" who had to be yet some product "of Ignorance and Superstition"; to what good these symbols, "vain remembrances of an age of slavery and obscurantism"? And they have erased the Great Architect from the boards and diplomas, and they have reduced the symbols to the intelligence of the pub regulars charged to explain them.

The foreign plan was thus realized. These "free men," these "beings of brilliant and enlightened reason," have been presented to the rest of the world as scoundrels and men vile enough to scorn the Great Architect; and immediately, in all the lodges of the universe, the watchword has passed as rapid as lightning, and the doors have been closed, as by enchantment, upon the nose of the "French free thinkers" indignant to find everywhere "Masons still attached to the errors of the past."

The roguish French were made to play like children. Their relations with the rest of the Mas ∴ unions of the universe were cut for the vast majority. It remained to cut definitively every bond, in throwing what remained of the Scottish system into the same path.

The flight of the treasurers, a most fitting occurrence, completely ruined the Scottish Supreme Council which remitted its Lodges to the "Grand Loge Symbolique Ecossais," the child of the rebellion, and thus constituted the *Grand Lodge of France*, which, ever led in secret by intrigues, was eager to scratch the name of the G ∴ A ∴ which still attached some French to the foreigner.

There only remains some Scottish chapters and some rare areopagi capable of maintaining the bond with universal Masonry, and they work steadfastly to break this final cord.

But the invisible keep watch. These are the Illuminati who have made Masonry, and who have chosen France as the superior center in the Visible, as it is in the Invisible. It is also the Illuminati who will save once again the blind and the deaf.

May the members of the Scottish Supreme Council who read these lines reflect a little, and may they come out, for a moment from the narrow atmosphere of personal quarrels and questions of money.

The salvation of the patient work of their predecessors is in their hands, and our role must be limited to throwing up the cry of alarm.

As to the rest, they already know all this and we have nothing to teach them. We may have full and entire confidence in their clairvoyance and their patriotism.

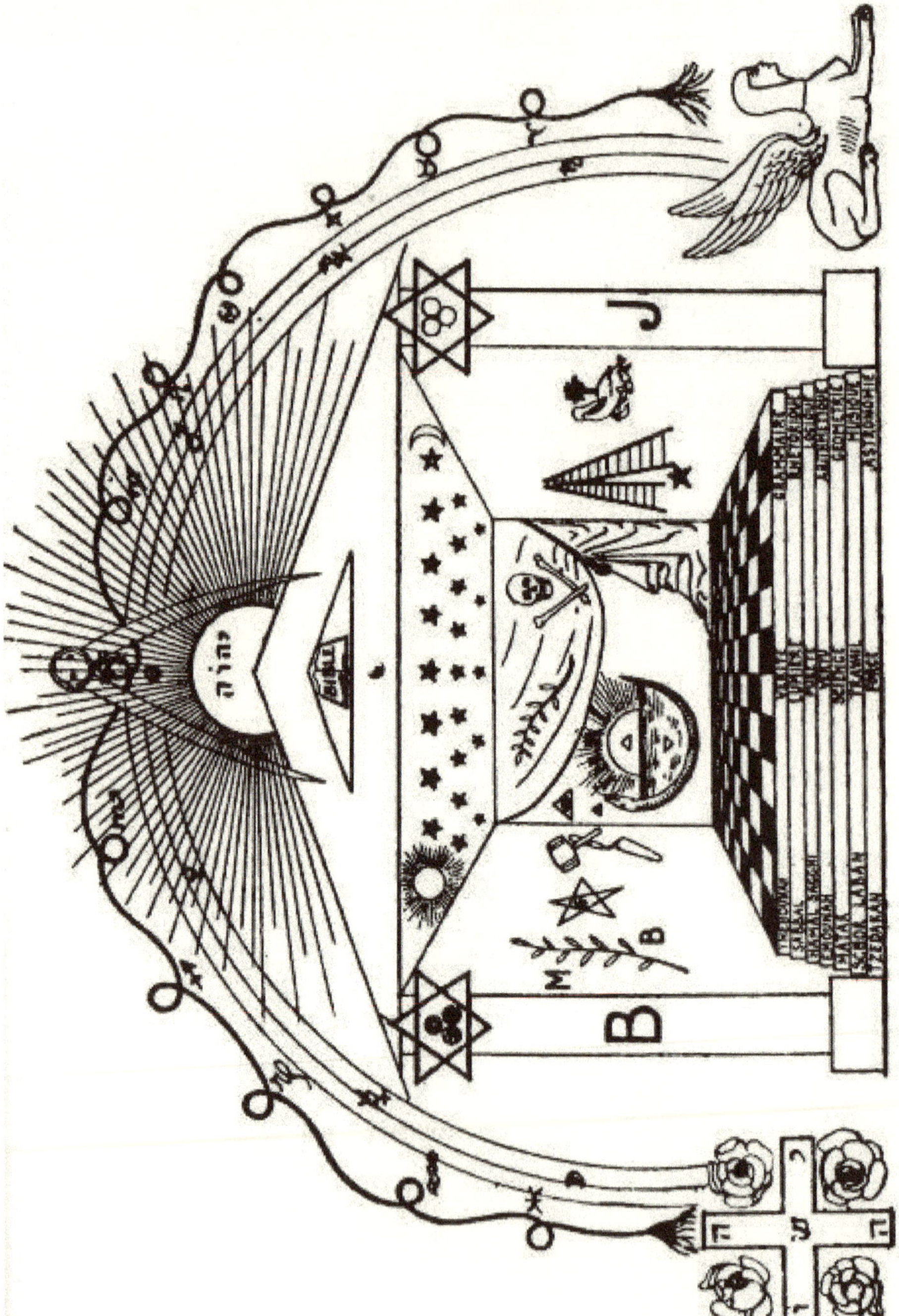
J
B
M
B
BIBLE

DISCOURSES ON MASONIC INITIATION

Discourse for the First Degree

My Brother,

You enter today into a new society. In the other societies presently organized in the civilized lands, they admit you; either directly or upon the presentation of sponsors, and without any special ceremony.

Among us, you have assisted in the ceremonies, in the trials, and in the interrogations, which must have seemed strange to you in an era as positive as ours. Instead of a bare room and of men presenting themselves to you as in civic life, you were surrounded by symbols: the men who presented themselves to you are adorned with symbolic ribbons, and the brothers who surround you likewise present you with objects being related to the trade of construction. All this has for its aim to show you, that from this day, you are called to the glorious, but sometimes difficult role of social constructor. Just as the ignorant, the sectarians, the half-educated men, will profess around you the destruction of all its forms, the Center into which you enter is going to teach you to distinguish what it is necessary to destroy, and what is necessary, on the contrary, to rebuild.

Materially, they have presented you a rough stone of which it will be necessary for you to round the corners, in order to do personal work. You have thus rough-hewn the stone, freed the future element of construction from the thorns and brambles which could surround it. You will present to the architect an element completely ready to enter into the edifice. But this construction, like all that surrounds you, is symbolic, and it is not in a quarry open to all the winds that you will have to construct your edifice, it is the human minds, in the hearts of men, which no longer receive the light of our apartments that you will have to manifest your action. But in order to do useful work, it is necessary that you be called progressively to wield the symbolic tools, which are placed in your hands. The level will no longer be but a sectarian instrument of destruction, unless its action is equilibrated by the rule; and the trowel will only be truly fruitful if it serves to manifest the plan of the architect. That is why several degrees exist in the instruction of the members of the great symbolic family.

Today, you are student-builder. Vested in a symbolic apron, you will listen and you will profit from acquiring it from those who preceded you in the quarry.

Tomorrow, conscious of your intellectual strength, having manifested your desire to pass from the material works to the works of the spirit, the traditional Science of Masonry will open for you its symbols and its books, in the second degree of our grades.

For the moment, the great family of brothers, known and unknown, is opened to you. Come to know the Masonic spirit, learn to remove from yourself the false knowledge of sectarianism, combat prejudice, enlighten every mind darkened by obscurantism, and be worthy to be one of these hidden lights who radiate in humanity.

Discourse for the Second Degree

Grade of Companion

My Brother,

As Apprentice, you had made three voyages. In the first, disorder reigned around you and you overcame various obstacles; in the second, a clanking of disquieting arms had stricken your ears, and when, after the third, the light was presented to you, you have seen your brothers armed and assembled, ready to protect you and defend you in the new path that you have followed.

After weeks of study, your mind was, little by little, freed from the prejudices and errors of profane society. You have learned to think for yourself; you have learned to express your thought and, conscious of your intellectual evolution, you are today worthy of an increase in salary.

In order to understand the mysteries of the second degree of the Masonic science, you have - like the ancient Companions - to accomplish several voyages.

First, armed with the instruments of demolition - a mallet and chisel - you have symbolically attacked the errors wherever they struck your conscience; then, holding the compass and the rule, you have begun to trace the board of your future works; then, thanks to the crow-bar and the rule, you have begun materially the construction of the edifice; finally, thanks to the rule and the square, you have been able to construct your edifice in a normal fashion and in a manner to defy time. Then the material work was ended.

In the fifth voyage, you no longer had any material tool, and it is the intellectual tradition that you have come to request of us.

Formerly, the free men, wishing to think freely, were oppressed by the tyrannical organizations of the powers or of the priesthoods. It is then that some proud souls founded these associations of initiated laity who, in imitation of the great Egyptian fraternities, established in all the land a mysterious bond, uniting the intelligences outside of nationalities, religions, and sects. Certain signs, known only by the brethren, allowed them to communicate between themselves in a discreet fashion, and to be recognized in profane society. It is thanks to the knowledge of these signs that Plato was freed from slavery by a brother that he had encountered. It is thanks to these mysterious fraternities that after the occupation of Egypt by Rome, the initiated laity, the descendants of the Pythagoreans, later the Essenes, have preserved upon the earth this invisible chain connecting between them the men freed from servitude.

Uniting among themselves, these brothers received the new brothers as formerly they were received in the temples of Egypt.

Aside from the visible light, they learned the existence of an invisible light, source of unknown forces and energies - that secret light which enlightens every man coming into this world and which was represented by the star with five branches, symbol of man radiating mysterious light and thus constituting this marvelous emblem of the blazing star!

My brother, you are going to study the history of the tradition of these ancient fraternities. To understand the Masonic science, you must penetrate intellectually into these ancient mysteries. You must discover the bond which, since the temples of Thebes, across the Pythagorean fraternities, the Essenes, the first Johannites, the brothers escaped from Constantinople to the fall of that city, descends unto us through the Troubadours, the free-judges, the alchemists, the Templars, the Illuminati, and the modern Masonic rites.

Do not neglect, my brother, this intellectual study. Without this work, which ought to be your personal work, Freemasonry would remain for you misunderstood and as a closed book. Apart from some rare brothers, who will put their knowledge at your disposal, the lodge will be of little use to you from this point of view.

You have been guided up to the present; begin to walk alone. Educate yourself in a positive manner and you will then be a true blazing star, shedding the acquired light upon the brethren and the profane who will call out to your devotion and your knowledge.

Discourse for the Third Degree

Grade of Master

First Part
Before the Initiation

My Brother,

When you requested to take part in Freemasonry, you remained for a certain moment in a chamber where the symbol was manifested to you in various manners. It is in dying to prejudices, obscurantism, all the ancestral or social errors, that you are become Freemason.

Today, your sustained work, your zeal for the Order, your devotion to your brothers, permits us to call you to the participation of the more profound mysteries and to initiate you to the degree of Master. This degree is perhaps the one which represents most marvelously of all the ancient mysteries of Egypt.

Formerly, the initiate to the mysteries of Osiris learned, beyond the existence of the mysterious forces that the degree of Companion has revealed to you, the possibility for man to live a life different from the physical life. They taught him that the coming and going of terrestrial existence are guarded by the terrible mystery of death; and, in order to express this mystery symbolically, the initiate was surrounded by bandelets, placed in a coffin, and the mortuary songs were raised sad and majestic around him, then he was reborn. A new light was revealed to him and his mind, made dynamic by the terror conquered by death, was opened to more noble ideas, to more sublime devotions.

Today, the profane sciences, thanks to the dedication of the brothers who have preceded us, have transformed social life. The handling of the physical forces is come out of the ancient universities, from the closed temples, in order to enter into the laboratories, and like the symbolic pelican who gives its blood to feed its offspring, like the contemporary scholar, the true seer into a humanity still blind, dispenses to the profane his knowledge and devotion.

But the tradition of symbols is also a living science. It allows the one who possesses it to adapt his knowledge to the needs of his brothers, to raise again a society which is collapsed, to sustain a heart in courage and to project the light where darkness would reign in mastery.

Formerly, they related to the initiate the history of Osiris, his rending, his reconstitution by Isis, and the symbolic dances of the initiators revealed the mysteries that the word was incapable of translating.

Each teaching center possessed a symbolic history - legend

frivolous in appearance for the initiates - which served as the basis of all teaching on the mysteries.

Freemasonry, direct heir of these ancient initiatic fraternities, have not failed in this duty. We are going to related to you, my brother, the legend of Hiram, and if we had not seen to precede this account by the considerations that we just developed, this legend would appear to us as a banal narrative of ancient things of little interest, and your attention would not be incited to break the husk of the legend, in order to find in the center of the fruit the nutritious kernel, liberator of your intellectuality.

The legend of Hiram contains the key of the greatest symbolic adaptations that the Masonic Order may have to fulfill. From the social point of view, the adaptation of the intelligence to the various genres of labors, the division of the social forces concurrent to the harmony of all, the place given to the master by his knowledge are developed here. From the moral point of view, the terrible law which sees that the one that you have sustained, that you have instructed, that you have saved, has revolted against you and seeks to kill you, according to the formula of the human animal "the initiate will kill the initiator" is taught there. Practically, at last, the certainty that every sacrifice is the key of a future flowering, the branch of acacia which will guide the brothers to the tomb of the one who has been sacrificed for them, all this is eternally living for a mind to comprehend, and indicates a teaching which may always be transmitted across humanity, whatever be the evolution of profane society.

That our old brothers of the 18th century have seen in this legend a mythic representation of the march of the sun, that others have discovered therein philosophical adaptations, this matters little, for every truly symbolic legend is a universal key, adaptable to all the physical, mental, and spiritual manifestations.

Now, my brother, you understand the raison d'être of the mysteries in which you are going to participate, and you know why Freemasonry must respect the tradition and the symbols which have been confided to its master initiators.

Discourse for the Third Degree

Grade of Master

Second Part
After the Initiation

From this day, you are a true link in the universal chain constituted over all the Earth by Freemasonry. From this day, you will participate in the gatherings of the middle chamber where the architects of the future society are assembled physically or mystically in order to give to humanity each day, a little more light, a little more well-being, and a little more reason.

Participating in the universal work of Freemasonry, you have the right of assistance in the entire universe. Wherever you are, whatever be the opinions of the people among whom you will stay, whatever be their language, make a sign and our brothers will hasten to you.

You have triumphed over death. New Hiram of the social annunciation, you are now going to establish consciously the plan of your intellectual monument, for you are no longer the Apprentice who strove painfully to polish a badly cut stone; you are no longer the Companion who, strong in intellectual teachings and Masonic traditions, had constituted his cerebral dynamism; you are the Master, conscious of your personality, called to exercise, in the Order, all the administrative functions of the lodges, called to direct the Apprentices in their intellectual research, and your colleagues - the Masters - in the tracing of their symbolic boards.

Your responsibility increases in the same proportion as the extent of your functions. If the Order assures you, everywhere, passage and protection, it expects of you a continued effort, a labor without weakness for the liberation of the oppressed intelligences, and a courage in every trial, if it is necessary to risk something in order to save one of your brothers.

Spread everywhere, then, the light that you have received; seek in profane society the free intelligences, the elevated hearts, the adventurous spirits who, fleeing the shackles, the easy life, and the prejudices, seek a new life and are able to be powerful elements for the diffusion of the Masonic ideas. Learn to direct yourself, to flee all sectarianism; and if you combat the errors and superstition that the various priesthoods impose on a humanity still in infancy, know always how to be tolerant; do not become yourself a sectarian odious to the humans.

Philosopher, that is to say friend of wisdom, know always how to keep the mental equilibrium which characterizes the man sound of mind. Recall that Hiram placed its two columns and that the capital of the entrance of the temple rests harmoniously, supported by Jakin and Bohaz, that is to say by strength and beauty.

An edifice is not constructed in being supported upon a sole column; know, therefore, in the intellectual construction that you will have to undertake, how to always equilibrate the teachings of the reason by the devotions of the heart. Recall that Freemasonry comes to the aid of the misfortunate, whatever be their opinions; that, in its action upon profane society, it frees the conscience as well as it raises the courage of those who no longer hope; and if, in life, those treacherous wish to make your work disappear, if, new Hiram, you are at the point of receiving the fatal blow of the mallet on the part of the unconscious or revolted, recall that all the brothers here present will defend you. Recall that dedicated Masters will seek, later, the trace of your works, and that the branch of acacia will serve to recognize your efforts in view of the development of our Order and of the manifestation of your intellectual efforts.

Work, my brother; become aware of your new duties; and if ever discouragement enters into your soul, if your spirit loses the strength to fight, remember this solemn day and say, at the moment when the flesh leaves the bone: "No! I will not fail in my mission; No! Cowardice will not enchain my spirit; No! I will not be stopped in my mission of progress, for the acacia is known to me.

SYMBOLS OF FREEMASONRY

The Legend of Hiram

The acacia is known to me!

The symbols of the Occult Science, preserved unto our day by Freemasonry, may be divided into two classes:

The ones, like the tableaux of the lodges, the hieroglyphs, the colors, the ceremonies are not understood by the majority of the affiliates but in their most base sense, when they are understood at all.

The others, contained within some narratives like those of the death of Hiram or of J.-B. Molay, are still understood in several of their significations.

It is with one of these last symbols, the legend of Hiram, that we are going to occupy ourselves.

The origin of this legend is rather interesting, for it marks the real origin of modern Freemasonry. Here it is according to Ragon:

"This same year (1646) a society of the Rose Croix, formed according to the ideas of the *New Atlantis* of Bacon, assembled in the meeting room of the Freemasons at London. Ashmole and the other brothers of the Rose-Croix, having recognized that the number of workers of the trade were surpassed by that of the workers of intelligence, because the first were growing weaker each day, while the latter increased continually, thought that the moment had come to renounce the formulas of reception of these workers, which consisted only in some ceremonies pretty much similar to those utilized among the trade folk, which had, until then, served as shelter to the *initiates* to be joined with the *adepts*.

"They substituted them, with the means of the oral traditions that they used for their aspirants to the Occult Sciences, a written mode of initiation calculated on the ancient mysteries, and on those of Egypt and Greece, and the first initiatic grade was written such, pretty much as we know it. The first degree having received the approval of the initiates, the grade of Companion was drafted in 1648; and that of Master a little while after. But the decapitation of Charles I in 1649 and the side that Ashmole took in favor of the Stuarts, brought great modifications to this third and final grade, become biblical, all while leaving for its basis that great hieroglyph of nature symbolized towards the end of December.[10]"

This seems, at first sight, to contradict certain of my former assertions on the subject of the origin of the Masonic doctrine[11]; but in reflecting a little it is easy to see therein, on the contrary, the confirmation of my words.

What is, indeed, the series by which this new society of 1648 attaches itself to the ancient occult science on the one hand, and to the Templars on the other?

Read the biography of Ashmole and you are going to find in this admirable man an erudite Egyptologist and even better a remarkable Hermeticist, a descendant of John Dee, the alchemist of London, author of the Monas Hieroglyphica.

Ashmole is an initiate of the alchemists, and as such he wielded the symbol in a masterly manner.

See, on the other hand, this mention of the Rose-Croix, the true ones, those who preceded the birth of Freemasonry, and you will recognize effortlessly in them those mysterious unknowns that the "brothers" would so despise later.

We do not deviate, however, from the subject which interests us, and we return to the legend of Hiram, of which we know the principal author, Elias Ashmole.

How is the legend of Hiram distinguished from some fairy tale, and why can we designate it under the name of symbolic history?

A symbolic history is a combined history of such kind that the evolution of the personages indicates exactly the evolution of Nature.

Modern mythologies have had a good hand in showing that all the histories which are connected to the Hindu, Egyptian, Greek, and Roman divinities, and even to the Christ of the Christians, were only more or less perfect pictures of the march of the Sun. From this, the name of solar myths is given to all these accounts.

This is true, on the condition of not seeing there exclusively this astronomical meaning, and the method of the Occult Science, Analogy, is going to completely enlighten us on this subject.

The legend of Hiram being a symbolic history, let us look at the raison d'être of this genre of symbol, and we can all the better understand the developments that we will draw therefrom later on.

If it is true that one same law governs all the phenomena of Nature, to expose one of these phenomena, is to expose all the others. That is the basis of analogy.

Let us take three examples in order to explain this: the evolution of a grain of wheat, the march of the sun, the manufacturing of the philosopher's stone, and let us look at whether these three things are not governed by the same law.

The grain of wheat is destined to produce an entire stalk. Scarcely is it planted in the earth that a violent struggle is engaged between the germ that it contains and the exterior elements. One moment all is rotten, the grain of wheat seems dead forever; it is precisely at this moment that it is more living than ever. From the midst of this decay, from this darkness, from this chaos, is raised a new being, directing itself towards the light. The grain of wheat has just made itself immortal in the numerous shoots that it is going to produce.

The sun is destined to give life to all the planetary beings which gravitate around it, as well as to what covers them.

Scarcely has it begun its fecundating course that a violent struggle is engaged upon the earth between its good influences and the hoar-frost. Winter soon triumphs.

Most beneficent sun, it is perhaps dead forever!

It is, however, when death seems to triumph over advantage that life possesses its greatest strength. Winter, proud of its cruelty, believes to be forever the master, when the child who lies hidden under its shroud triumphs in the end, and winter flees astonished before the radiant springtime which rises up, immortalizing everywhere the germs through procreation.

The philosopher's stone is destined to produce the great work of man. Scarcely will the elements which constitute it be present in the athanor that a violent struggle breaks out among them. The beautiful colors disappear and the mass seems forever rotten, all is black like the head of a crow. It is then that the ignorant are desolate and that the wise rejoice. From the midst of this chaos comes at the end of some time the dazzling whiteness, the indicator of life. The colors appear progressively; the elements of the stone have just made themselves immortal in the transmutations that they will produce.

It is not difficult to find in these three phenomena one same law, that of the struggle of life against death, of which one may thus announce the phases!

First phase:

The struggle is established between life and death. Life is weaker and yields to death.

Progressive Materialization. - The grain of wheat rots. - Autumn appears with the hoar-frost. - The colors of the work are altered.

Second phase:

Death seems triumphant. It is then that life fights with more strength.

Equilibrium between the Materialization and the Spiritualization. - The germ lies hidden under the putrefaction. - Winter shelters the children of spring. - Dazzling colors are going to come out of the darkness.

Third phase:

Life triumphs in its turn. Death is conquered anew.

Progressive Spiritualization. - The stalk appears. - Spring manifests. - The beautiful colors of the stone show themselves.

If, therefore, we wish to relate this marvelous law in a history, we will speak of a wise, strong, or virtuous man killed by some villainy, of the triumphal resurrection of the good, and of the punishment of the guilty.

The scholar will wish to see only the history of a cycle of the Sun, and will scoff at the protestations of the alchemist asserting that it is a question of the philosopher's stone. It is a question of all this and much more besides in these symbolic histories; and the true Rose-Croix to whom they have asked for the key of the Great Work of Nature are content to show the twelfth key of the universal book in explaining it thus:

One must know hot to die in order to be reborn immortal.

In the ancient Egyptian initiations, when the veil which hid the sanctuary came to be lowered before the profane, the candidate assisted in a strange scene. The high priest related to him anew that history of the murder of Osiris that every Egyptian knew from his childhood; but the future initiate guessed, by this new manner of setting forth the legend, a mysterious side unseen by him until then. Soon the trials of the psychic initiation were going to enlighten him further.

"In Egypt, the 3rd grade is called *Door of death.* The coffin of Osiris which, because of his *supposed recent* assassination, still bore traces of blood, was raised in the middle of the room of the dead, where it was made a part of the reception. They asked the assistant if he had taken part in the murder of Osiris; after other trials and despite his denials, he was stricken or one feigned to strike him on the head with the blow of an axe. He was thrown down, covered by bandages like the mummies; they moaned around him; shone lights; the supposed dead was surrounded by fire, then restored to life."[12]

In the modern Masonic initiation, the candidate, be he a worthy commoner or a professor of the college of France, is no less astonished at hearing related the history of the murder of the biblical blacksmith. The meaning of the symbolism is unknown to such a degree in our era that the spirit is disconcerted before these rites which, though admirably conceived, pass for ridiculous. Without wishing, however, to remain any further on this point, let us approach this legend, in order to then seek there the various meanings most easily discovered.

∴

Solomon, wishing to raise a temple to the Eternal, asked for the support of his neighbor, the king of Tyre. This latter sent him the most able of his workers, among others, the man charged to direct the labors of the Temple, with an architect named Hiram.

This was a man as fierce as he was educated. Raised in the middle of the wild forests, Nature was his sole director. He penetrated its most profound mysteries by the sole force of his marvelous intuition.

From his arrival, Hiram portioned the workers into three great classes: to his right, he arranged those who worked the wood; to his left, those who were occupied with metals; finally, in the middle were found those who worked the stone.

When the division by classes, according to the profession, was accomplished, Hiram divided each of the classes into three parts, according to the knowledge of – those who comprised them.

The less educated constituted in each class the Apprentices; those who were skilled in the works that they carried out were the Companions; finally, those who directed the others were the Masters.

In order to prevent any confusion between these orders, each of the members received a mysterious word indicating his place in the hierarchy; the Apprentices were recognized by pronouncing the word *Jakin*, the Companions by saying *Bohaz*; the Masters by spelling the mysterious tetrad of the initiates: IHVH.

Such is the admirable order according to which the wise Hiram established his hierarchy.

Knowledge alone permitted the workers to rise a rank, but this wise measure was nevertheless the cause of the murder of Hiram.

Three wicked companions wanted to extract by force from the great architect of the Temple the mysterious word of the Masters and concocted to this end the most infamous plot. The Masters were gathered each day in a chamber situated in the middle of the temple, and the door situated at the East was reserved to them. This wise Hiram came out last of all, after assuring himself of the good execution of his orders.

Knowing this peculiarity, the three Companions lay in wait for the exit of the great architect. Hiram, the works of the day accomplished, goes to the door of the South, where he finds *Jubelas* who demands from him the Masters' word. With his habitual gentleness, Hiram pointed out to the Companion that knowledge alone permitted one to know the mysterious formula. The Companion wanted to strike Hiram on the head with the heavy iron rule of twenty-four inches with which he was armed. The master deflected the blow and is struck only at the throat.

Hiram returned then to the door of the West which served as common entrance to all the workers. There, *Jubelos* was found who, upon the refusal of the master to deliver his secret, struck him at the heart with his heavy square.

Completely stunned, Hiram dragged himself to the door of the East, where *Jubelum*, rendered even more furious than his accomplices by the refusal of the architect, achieved a mallet blow upon the forehead.

The three villains were interrogated mutually, and seeing that their plan had run aground, no longer had but one desire: to make the traces of their crime disappear.

They hid the corpse in the debris, and the next day, at first light, carried it into a neighboring forest, where they buried it.

A branch of acacia alone indicated the tomb of the greatest of men.

However, Solomon, not seeing his architect return, and having a presentiment of misfortune, sent at first three Masters to his search. These latter having found nothing, the king sent anew nine Masters who, at the end of seven days of searching, discovered, by the branch of acacia, the tomb of Hiram, who lives again, thanks to them, in each true Freemason.

The guilty who had escaped were taken without delay. Their retreat was betrayed by an unknown and one of the twelve Masters sent to punish them killed the most guilty among them, the assassin of Hiram, *Abibala*, in a cavern near a spring where he took refuge.

A dog indicated the place of retreat of the villain. The other assassins were killed by hurling themselves from the height of the quarries in which they took refuge. The heads of the three Companions were brought to Solomon.

∴

Such is in its principal lines, the legend of Hiram. Before undertaking the study of the various senses in which one may consider it, I must make some important remarks.

First of all, it has seemed to me useless to complicate this narrative by this introduction of the embellishments with which the imagination of the fabricators of rituals have adorned it. Thus, some authors mix with this legend the account of the loves of Hiram with Balkis, queen of Sheba, and have Solomon enter as an accomplice in the murder of Hiram.

Another rather curious remark, is the changes of the names of the three villains in the various degrees. Thus the reader has without doubt seen with astonishment *Jubelum* become *Abibala* shortly before his death.

Here is what the *Thuiler general* says on the subject:

"The names of the three murderers of Hiram vary much in the different degrees, and according to the diverse applications that are made of Masonry. They are:

Abiram, Romvel, Gravelot,

or Habblen, Schterke, Austersfurth,

or Giblon, Giblas, Giblos,

or Jubela, Jubelo, Jubelum, etc.

"The Templar sees here *Squin de Florian, Noffodei,* and the *Inconnu* [Unknown] on the depositions of whom Philip the Fair accused the Order before the Pope, or even the three abominables, Philip the Fair, Clement V, and Noffodei.

"The crowned Mason, the Rose-Croix of France, substitutes them

Judas, Caiaphas, and Pilate, the three authors of the death of Jesus.

"In the Rose-Croix of *Kulwining* the three assassins of beauty are: Cain, Hakan, Heni."

Let us say, finally, that the death of the three villains is recounted differently in the various rites. The form of the rest matters little, the basis alone is what interests us in the developments which are going to follow.

Like all the symbolic histories, the legend of Hiram contains several meanings which may be classified into three groups: natural, moral, and psychical.

1.   *Natural meaning.* - In the natural or physical sense, the legend may be considered under two principal aspects: as social, being applied to the laws of society; and as astronomical, developing a solar myth.

Let us consider somewhat the manner by which Hiram divided his workers and we will see appear one of the most beautiful social ideas that one may develop. What protestation against those societies where intrigue alone leads to all! There must be none idle in the work undertaken by Hiram: all are workers. Understanding however, that the liberty of man must be respected before all, Hiram left each to take up in Society the work that he can lead to a good end, and proclaim, from the basis of his organization, the principle: *To each according to his aptitude.*

The classes once established, at the number of three, the social hierarchy made its appearance. Everywhere and always there will be found directors and the directed; it is a natural law that planets gravitate around a sun, and this law is observed analogically as much in the course of a family as in that of the Universe.

Here the satellites obey the solar impulse; there, the children must bend to the parental impetus.

What, then, is the means established by Hiram to become a member of the directing class?

Is it the inheritance of titles and feudal charges? No.

Is it the inheritance of fortune, submitting the poor to the despotism of an immoral and degenerate being? No.

Is it intrigue giving place to the most protected? No, a thousand times no. Nothing prevents the one who wishes to see himself attain to the first rank, in the Society of Hiram. It suffices to be worthy of it.

All to merit and not to inheritance, all to knowledge and not to fortune, all to concourse and not to intrigue, such is the expression of the second social formula of Hiram.

To all those who claim that Freemasonry is not attached to any filiation, show the legend of the Master. If they deny the possible existence of an ideal society in which only those who know lead, recount to them with Fabre d'Olivet and Saint-Yves d'Alveydre the history of Ram and his universal empire; if the past no longer interest them, transport them to the heart of the institutions of venerable China and seek with them the employ which is not gained in competition.[13]

We may show again other social developments in this legend, but we lack the space. Let it suffice us to indicate and understand the first two social formulas of Hiram.

First, to each according to his aptitude; then, to each according to his merit.[14] The astronomical sense has been treated with enough authority by all the Masonic authors that I believe it useless to add anything thereto. It is as solar myth that the affiliates consider nearly exclusively the legend of Hiram, witness the following extract:

"The sun, at the summer solstice, provokes, among all that breathes, the songs of rebirth; then Hiram who represents it, may give, to whom has the right, the sacred word, that is to say life.

"When the sun descends into the inferior signs, the mutism of nature begins; Hiram may no longer give the sacred word to the Companions who represent the last three inert months of the year.

"The first Companion is reputed to strike Hiram weakly with a rule of twenty- four inches, image of the 24 hours that each diurnal revolution lasts: first distribution of time which, after the exaltation of the great star, waits feebly its existence, in bearing upon it the first blow.

"The second strike by the *iron square*, symbol of the final season, represented in the intercession of two straight lines which divided into four equal parts, the zodiac circle, the center of which symbolizes the heart of Hiram, where ends the point of the four squares representing the four seasons: second distribution of time which, in this era, bears a greater blow to the solar existence.

"The third Companion strikes him mortally on the forehead *by a blow of the mallet*, whose cylindrical form symbolizes the year [année] which means circle, anneau [ring]: third distribution of time, the accomplishment of which bears the final blow to the existence of the *expiring* sun.

"In this interpretation, they have concluded that Hiram, founder of metals, become the hero of the new legend with the title of *architect* is the *Osiris* (the sun) of modern initiation; that Isis, his widow, is the *Lodge* (emblem of the earth) in Sanskrit, *Loga*, the world; and that Horus, son of Osiris (or of the light) and son of the widow is the Freemason, that is to say the *initiate* who inhabits the terrestrial lodge (child of the widow and of the light)."[15]

"Thus the three perfidious Companions betray their master, as did Typhon in regards to Osiris, and they say in the narration: Hiram presents himself at the door of the West in order to leave the temple: this is precisely what the sun does; for, if I suppose this star taking its domicile in the sign of the ram, on the first day of spring, the last day of its triumph at the summer solstice, or the vigil of its death, which has taken place in the

Balance, it descends to the horizon by the door of the West. And if I then examine the position that the ram takes at the East, I will see close to it the great Orion, arms raised, holding a club, in the position to strike it. To the north, I will see Perseus, a weapon in hand and in the position of a man ready to make an evil blow. I repeat, the assassination of Hiram, taken in the figurative or allegorical style, is like the passion of Osiris, as that of Adonis, Atys, and Mithra, a deed of the imagination of astronomer priests, who had for their aim the portraiture of the absence of the sun upon the earth.

"The romance that they have presented us on Hiram is complete, for the heavens also let us see *the nine masters* who went to search for his body; and if one carries his gaze to the West of the horizon, when the sun is set in the ram, one will see around this constellation Perseus, Phaeton, and Orion.

"By following in this way the constellations which decorate the sky in this position, one will note, to the north, Cepheus, Hercules, and Bootes, and to the East, one will see appear the Centaur, the Serpent-eater, and the Scorpion; all progressing with it, and following it step by step until the moment of its new appearance in the East."[16]

2. *Moral sense.* - The moral and religious sense of the Legend of Hiram has been undertaken by all the great reformers of Freemasonry. Thus, in an essay on the unification of the various rites, entitled the *Master decorated in three points*, the candidate consulted on the secret of the order, divides it into five distinct parts.

"The first part has a relation to the exposition of the *natural, universal, and immutable religion* by means of the symbols and maxims."

The legend of Hiram, by the effort of all his workers of classes and foreign nationalities, contributing by their works to raise the Temple of the only God, teaches to all its adepts the tradition of the Gnostics and of the ancient initiates; the existence of the only Religion, of which all the cults are manifestations.

It is because of this that the true Freemason must be the enemy of sectarianism, whatever form it may take.

The second part of the Masonic secret, according to the author that I just cited, is connected to the secret of the operations of nature.

This alludes to the *Hermetic* and *alchemical* meaning of the legend of Hiram of which I do not wish here to undertake the development.

The third part of the secret is the perfection of the human heart, of which the temple is but an allegory.

One could attach at this point of application, in the legend of Hiram, the great law of compensation represented by the resurrection of Hiram, the exile and punishment of the guilty.

How often does one not rise up against the maxim become

popular: *Vice is always punished and virtue rewarded?*

However, has not the knowledge of the law of Karma come to give an immense support to this maxim, in showing that, in the invisible, *an action solicits an equal reaction*, and in proclaiming the similitude of the moral laws?

The fourth part of the secret is related to the solar myth on which we have already spoken.

Finally, the fifth part retraces the struggle of the instincts and the will:

"The victory of the errors and passions over the truth, or of virtue over the errors and passions, represented equally by the death and resurrection of Hiram (who is the truth or virtue), who is stricken by three villainous Companions (*who are ambition, falsehood, and ignorance*), drawn from t:he tomb and avenged by nine virtuous Masters (who are the Masonic virtues and duties)."

3.   *Psychical sense.* - The most important of the meanings that one may attribute to the legend of Hiram is, without contradiction, that which has treated on the mysterious trials practiced in all the sanctuaries with a view to the development of the soul of the candidate.

The entire aim of the legend is found contained in this death of the righteous, killed in secret, and in his dazzling resurrection.

The principle of the Universe which presides over the destruction and the changing of the forms, this principle known in all the theogonies and designated under the name of Shiva, Ahriman, Typhon, Nahash, and Satan, has been marvelously defined by Fabre d'Olivet: Destiny.

The most terrible weapon that Destiny may oppose to the divinely all-powerful Human Will, is Death. Initiation in every era has wished to arrive at one aim: to instruct man, and by this to render Destiny impotent in its attacks.

At each step, the candidate of the mysteries of Eleusis was threatened by Death, and it is only in showing that he was always ready to submit to it that he arrived at the final revelations.

One of the most terrible trials that he had to endure was the following:

Two glasses were placed before him.

The high priest said to him:

"Son of the Earth, one of these two glasses contains a terrible poison. If you truly believe in the beyond, if you have no fear of dying, choose one of these glasses and drink. May the Gods protect you!"

In case of refusal, the candidate was imprisoned until his death.

Plato became celebrated among the initiates for the courage he displayed in this trial.

The legend of Hiram shows us the development of this mystery in this sage who dies rather than give up his secret, and who lives again immortal.

With respect to the history of the grain of wheat, we have rather insisted on this fact that death always precedes the following life, so that one may see in the same law applied to the evolution of the soul only an analogical repetition of the same fact.

"In symbolic language, one commonly says that *Death is the door to Life*: a truth little known by those who possess the degree of Master, though the emblems placed before their eyes ought to have instructed them on it. One learns, by this figure, that fermentation, that putrefaction precedes the birth and gives it; that in the first condition, the second cannot take place; that, in a word, for the generation to be accomplished, it is necessary that the generative principles die, so to speak, that they are dissolved, disunited by the putrefaction. Indeed, without an internal and fermentative movement, without the separation, without the disintegration of the surrounding parts, how would the germ force its way through across the envelopes which hold it captive?"[17]

"In all the ancient mysteries, as in the Masonic initiation, the ceremonial of reception represented the revolutions of the celestial bodies and their fecundating action upon the earth. This ceremonial likewise alluded to the various purifications of the soul during its passage across the planets, where it donned more pure bodies as it approached its source, the uncreated Light. The priests, who presided over the initiation, attributed to it the virtue to exempt the soul of the initiate from various planetary migrations; this soul, at the death of the adept, passed directly into the abode of the eternal beatitude."[18]

All this appeared fabulous to more than one Freemason, if I have not taken care to cite the opinion of one of their most serious books: the *Thuiler général.*

Let us enter, however, into some details on the subject of this exposition of immortality in the legend of Hiram.

When the architect of the Temple is killed, the murderers bury it in the ground and mark the place of his tomb with a branch of Acacia. This is what will soon guide the Masters in their search. What, then, does this symbol represent?

The Acacia is the analogue of the Hawthorn, of the Egyptian and Christian Cross, and of the Hebrew letter Vav, which means Bond.[19]

This is the symbolism of the Bond which unites the Visible with the Invisible, our life to the following one; in a word, it is the promise of immortality.

The body of Hiram is in putrefaction; but over him is raised the dead branch, color of Hope, which indicates that all is not finished.

Let us now admire the genius of the authors of the legend, who put this symbol speaking in the mouths of all the Masters. The Freemason has in vain become atheist, no longer believing in the spiritual transformations of his being; he himself acknowledges, though unknown to him, his ignorance and proves that he understands nothing in the symbols when he says:

The acacia is known to me.[20]

If you understand immortality, you ask, then why profess materialism?

Freemasons who ridicule the Occult Science, Freemasons who ridicule the spiritualist theories, return to the Legend of the Great Architect of the mystical Temple; understand your symbols and you will see how ridiculous appear your positive formulas preferred before the *Blazing Star*!

You are to be enemies of all sectarianism, fear becoming sectarians yourselves.

We have just passed in review some of the meanings that the study of this admirable legend of Hiram may reveal to you.

Ashmole has changed into a branch of Acacia the ancient palm by which Homer and Virgil have endowed men twice-born: corporeally by terrestrial birth, spiritually by psychic initiation.

But whether it is a branch of Acacia, Olive, Myrtle, or of a Cross which is erected before the investigator, everywhere must be seen the same symbol of psychic rebirth to say with Ashmole and the Rose-Croix:

Immortality is known to me!

MASONIC REGULARITY

Repeatedly, our readers have been kept current, especially by the writings of Teder, on various points of history concerning the origin of the French Masonic Lodges. This study was made from the solely historical point of view, and outside of any questions of party.

Now, it is found that the illustrious descendants of Lacorne, who are no longer received in the English lodges, have come to place themselves as champions of a regularity all the more amusing that it is historically and documentarily one of the most problematic. Br.·. John Yarker has made on this subject, some studies which are an authority in the opinion of the writers on all the rites. Today we are happy to give a summary of an article full of enthusiasm and somewhat indignant by Br.·. Villarino del Villar, president of the Supreme Council of a Spanish rite which counts a multitude of lodges in Spain and warrants of amity in nearly all the lands of Europe.

It is with joy that we open our review to our Spanish BB.·. and that we put ourselves always at their disposal in order to propagate the good word and beautiful ideas.

We have respected in the translation all the terms of the original and one will recognize the effect of the beautiful Spanish sun in the indignant reprimands that unjustified attacks attach to the Castillan writer.

N.D.L.R.

Listen, Regulars of Quartier!

The hour has sounded when we are no longer to listen to prudence, and if, in the campaign that we begin today, you force us to go as far as will be necessary; if you do not listen to us and continue your insane work, it will not be our fault.

From now on, your proceedings authorize us not to keep any consideration for anything or for anyone; but, as we venerate with love, nearly with fanaticism, the sublime and secular Masonic institution, we will soften our argumentation. If you oblige us therein still, we will go as far as necessary; arms do not fail us, and we have more than sufficient data to respond to you.

And as nothing is more eloquent than numbers, we permit ourselves to secure them for ourselves, at the example of the International Bureau of Masonic Relations and of the Br.·. Quartier.

We borrow, then, the following interesting table from the Illustrious B.·. Quartier la Tente according to the Acacia.

So-called Regular Masonic Powers in Europe

	Names	Capitals	Founded	Lodges	Members
1.	United Grand Lodge of England	London	1717	2607	150,000
2.	United Grand Lodge of Ireland	Dublin	1730	450	15,000
3.	United Grand Lodge of Scotland	Edinburgh	1736	1012	50,000
4.	Grand Orient of France	Paris	1736	396	27,000
5.	Grand Orient of Holland	The Hague	1756	91	2,093
6.	National Grand Lodge of Sweden	Stockholm	1760	35	12,295
7.	Mother Grand Lodge of the Three Globes	Berlin	1744	137	14,856
8.	National Grand Lodge of German F.·.M.·.	Berlin	1770	128	13,099
9.	Eclectic Grand Lodge	Frankfort	1783	21	3,091
10.	Royal York Grand Lodge	Berlin	1798	69	6,838
11.	Grand Lodge of the Sun	Beiruth	1811	33	4,848
12.	Grand Lodge of Hamburg	Hamburg	1811	48	4,238
13.	Grand Lodge of Saxony	Dresden	1811	24	4,448
14.	Grand Lodge of France A.·.S.·.C.·.E.·.	Paris	1812	81	5,100
15.	Grand Orient of Belgium	Brussels	1836	19	(s)
16.	Swiss Grand Lodge *Alpine*	Zurich	1844	33	3,670
17.	Swiss Grand Lodge *La Bonne Harmonie*	Darmstadt	1846	8	750
18.	Mother Grand	Copenhagen	1858	29	4,500

	Lodge of Denmark				
19.	Grand Orient *Lusitano Unido*	Lisbon	1859	25	(s)
20.	Grand Orient of Italy	Rome	1861	195	(s)
21.	Group of 5 Independent Lodges	Leipzig	1883	5	1,381
22.	Symbolic Grand Lodge of Hungary	Budapest	1886	61	4,306
23.	Spanish Grand Orient	Madrid	1889	59	2,594
24.	National Grand Lodge of Norway	Christiana	1891	13	3,900
	Total = 24 Regular Powers with			5,579 Lodges	333,607 Members

And let no one open their mouth: These alone are the good ones, no more, no less.

What erudition! What veracity! What justice! Decidedly, the regulars write for the Chinese.

We write, ourselves, for all those who wish to read us. *The Official Statistics*, published since the beginning of the present century, form a total of 137,075 active lodges, with 18,732,184 brothers, 2,576,460 sisters, which gives in all 21,308,644 active members and an equal quantity of inactive or dormant members. We ask: Are the two statistics exact? If yes, we declare with bitterness and grief that the Masonry of the entire world has lost in five years, the enormous quantity of 131,486 lodges and 20,975,037 adepts. If we accept as infallible the version of Br.·. Quartier. Horrible deception! Cruel loss! But, let us recapitulate. Fortunately, there is nothing to it. We believe, on the contrary, that there is an increase in the lodges, with the only difference that 20,975,037 Masons are false, bad, imperfect, clandestine, and irregular, and 333,607, according to what they declare themselves, are perfect and regular.

Such are the veracity and modesty of the regulars. Nothing may be clearer and more precise; but as it is necessary to put the dots upon the i, so is it indispensible to put an end to such audacities and to combat them by solid reasoning and evident proofs. We respond, using our right of legitimate defense, to those who have declared themselves pontiffs and arbiters, have given or refused patents of regularity, have made certificates or established differentiations, have determined castes, families, groupings distinct from the greater family, whose power and importance were and are still in the human fraternity and internationalism. We have decided to refuse them these rights and these powers whatever happens! Evil and irregular

Masons!

What, then, may these insults, these heresies signify?

These are the eternal enemies of the light and of progress who proffer these insults, and the proof is that they alter the truth. I repeat, for those who believe themselves perfect Masons, it is more than insane, it is criminal and fratricide!

It would seem useless to give proof of this declaration, but the annual of the Br.·. Quartier la Tente publishes statistics *urbi et orbi*; it is just that the irregulars give them also.

We do not assert that all that we are going to cite is exact, for there is no *absolute* certainty, but we repeat, under the guarantee of their authors, what known persons have published, what we have read, and that we possess.

Europe

Name of Organization	Date of Foundation
Grand Lodge of the Canaries	1723
Grand Lodge of France	1725
Grand Lodge of Spain	1728
Grand Lodge of Sweden	1730
Grand Lodge of Naples	1731
Grand Lodge of Holland	1731
Grand Lodge of Russia	1731
Grand Lodge of Tuscany	1733
Grand Lodge of Bavaria	1733
Grand Lodge of Sardinia	1733
Grand Lodge of Piemont	1733
Grand Lodge of Savoy	1737
Grand Lodge of Portugal	1738
Grand Lodge of Egypt	1738
Grand Lodge of Prussia	1738
Grand Lodge of Smyrna	1738
Grand Lodge of Poland	1739
Grand Lodge of Berlin	1740
Grand Lodge of Hamburg	1740
Grand Lodge of Malta	1740
Grand Lodge of Bavaria	1741
Grand Lodge of Denmark	1742
Grand Lodge of Naples	1747
Imperial Supreme Council of Naples	1747
Grand Lodge of Norway	1747
Grand Lodge of Italy	1751

Grand Lodge of Hanover	1754
Grand Lodge of Holland	1756
Grand Lodge of Berlin	1760
Grand Lodge of Spain	1767
Grand Lodge of Berlin	1770
Grand Orient of France	1773
Eclectic Grand Lodge of Frankfort	1781
Orient of France – modified	1804
Grand Orient of Spain	1804
Grand Orient of Portugal	1805
Grand Orient of Spain	1811
Grand Lodge of Saxony	1811
Communion of Castille at Madrid	1814

Independent Grand Lodge of Seville.
Regional Grand Lodge Catatarra Balear.
Grand Lodge of Munster.
Grand Lodge simbolica espanola.
Regional Grand Lodge of Galaica.
Regional Grand Lodge of Cordoba.
Regional Grand Lodge of Murcia.
Grand Lodge of Romania.
National Grand Lodge of Egypt.
Supreme Council of Ireland.
Supreme Council of Misraim at Paris.
Supreme Council of Romania.
Supreme Council of Egypt.
Italian Supreme Council at Milan.
Supreme Council of Berlin.
Iberian General Grand Council.
Grand Orient of Egypt.
Portuguese Grand Orient.
Grand Orient Lucano.
Grand Lodges of Swedenborgians.

Total, to our knowledge, 60 Masonic Supreme Councils in Europe, with the same raison d'être, the same rights, the same origins, and the same ends as all, and having, moreover, a numerical superiority over the 24 Supreme Councils which consider themselves as the only regular ones!

Regulars!!!

What does this word mean?

What are the proofs, what are the merits, the conditions, and the rights of such a regularity?

What is its origin, human or divine?

What is or what are the hierarchies the pontiffs instituted, recognized, or accepted in order to admit or refuse the legality?

Who are the men who recognize this pontiff or submit to his laws?

When they will have responded to us in a satisfying fashion, we will submit ourselves to this Supreme Authority, we will respect it; but until that moment, we will discourse on the mad, the prideful, the pedants, and the slothful, those who warp and ridicule the large and fraternal spirit of Masonry, for we recognize no other source of constitutive right of modern Masonry, than that indicated by the initiative of the four lodges of London in 1717, or principles than those which have presided over the creation of the Masonic organisms until our day.

So as to follow our previous observations, let us continue, then, our argumentation by giving the following teachings that have furnished us the world-wide statistics.

Different lands.

Names of the Supreme Councils:

Grand Lodge and Supreme Council of India.

Grand Lodges of Bengal, Massachusetts, Georgia, Boston, Cabo Coast, San Cristobal, Martinique, South Carolina, Jamaica, Isla Real, Santo Domingo, Madras, Pennsylvania, Guernessey, Jersey, Barbados, Guadeloupe, San Eustaquio, Nova Scotia, New Granada, Virginia, Terranova, Java, Dutch Guyana, Ceylon, Sumatra, Bermuda, Isla Borbon, Sarrate, Raleigh, Richmond, Isla del Principe de Gales, Cabo del Buena Esperanza, Vermont, Luisitania, Macao, New Jersey, Charleston, Maryland, New York, Connecticut, New Hampshire, Rhode Island, Santa Elena, Kentucky, Persia, Tennessee, Honduras, San Vincente, Maine, Pondichery, Bombay, Alabama, Mexico, Haiti, Michigan, French Guyana, Nouvelle-Galles, Honida, Australia, Arkansas, Boston, Peru, Texas, Illinois, Mozambique, Goa, Wisconsin, Jowa, California, Minnesota, Colorado, Chile, West Virginia, Montana, Nevada, Idaho, Quebec, Manitoba, Prince Edward, Colon & Cuba, New Mexico, New Brunswick, Tuner, Nacional de Cuba, Havana, Liberia, Supreme Council of Siberia, Supreme Council of Persia, Grand Orient of North America, Supreme Council of South America and the West, Grand Orient of the Blue Rite at Buenos Aires and

Confederated Lodges of Argentina.

Total, to our knowledge and except error, 115 superior organisms of Masonry.

Is it that all these supreme organisms were not created regularly in admitting that they did not have the incontestable right to make it with or without the good pleasure, the intervention, or the official authorization of the United Grand Lodge of England, to which we recognize fertile propaganda, initiatives, protections, by which it seconded the noble intentions of the celebrated Saint Paul Lodge of London?

Is it by chance (and we assert the contrary) that four-fifths of the organizations cited would have ceased to exist?

This would be truly sad, for then our enemies would have reason to assert and to support that Masonry no longer has any reason to be in our era, whereas all the Masons believe firmly that Masonry will only finish with the World and Humanity.

Not only do we believe, but we assert, in basing ourselves on certain proofs, that a great number of superior organisms continue to form (ten new for one that disappears). What, then, do these words mean: regular or irregular? Do they wish to attain to the Machiavellian *Divide*? Do they want to install the red pope?

Do they pretend to impose upon universal Masonry the adoption of a unique rite, perhaps the one of the Jew Morin? Impossible!

The present Masons are not some automatons, and do not accept what is imposed on them. They have nothing in common with wind-sails, do not let themselves be impressed by the wisdom of Solomon, have no enthusiasm for the legislation attributed to Frederick the Great. The modern Masons feel, think, discuss, write, read, and study, and all, basing themselves on reason and positive teachings, possessing origins without phantasmagoria or falsehoods, and acting accordingly, opt for what pleases them, create what seems to them most profitable, according to the era or the needs of each land, and rejecting the improbable and ridiculous.

As to you, regulars, your vanity, your pedantry, have produced the trouble and diminished the number of the adepts. For every individual who came to the Order had as an article of faith, that Masonry represented love, peace, true fraternity, justice, equity, the universe without frontier, humanity without privilege, nor difference of class, race, color, language or belief. But you wise and perfect Masons, you have decided otherwise. You have replaced love with hate, peace with war, fraternity with the oath; you have established a lame justice, you have transformed equity into caprice and internationalism, you understand it in your fashion. By your private initiative, you have created castes; for it is this that the words regular or irregular mean - good and bad Masons - as if you had the gift to know men, whereas nobody even knows how to understand himself. Your noisy fall could not be more immediate, more visible, for you cannot claim but twenty-four Masonic entities, quite debatable (especially the ones that we have the misfortune to know); do not claim that you consider yourselves as the sole and true Masons, for the statistics are crushing for you, and the results ought to serve as lesson and conclusive proofs to you. *Your anathemas do not frighten us.*

They say of the repented that they are the joy of heaven; but truly if you persist in your pretentious suicide, it will be necessary for someone to take the initiative to put an end to such arrogance and madness. If you persist, I repeat, all the energy that you have found to despise the excommunications of the Roman Church and the persecutions of the tyrants, we will oppose it to your audacities, even not knowing exactly what the aim is pursued by you. We know at least that, far from defending the purity of the principles, you seem determined to oppose yourselves to the development of the true Masonic Institution. The ideal is not the exclusive inheritance of anyone, know this well. In order to do good, shed the light, remember the truth, and exact justice, there is no need of trade- marks, and no one can restrain the free will and the incontestable right that we all possess to act when our actions do not harm others. Fortunately, all the institutions and all the peoples have their laws and live together on the basis of an established and shared right.

When, where, how, and for what have been instituted the general law and the international Masonic right?

The Convent of Lausanne in 1875, established the organic foundations for the Scottish Rite. Why, then, have those who observe or say they observe the said Rite not respected and do not respect the contract of Lausanne? And has not the legislation of the other Rites the right to respect, though no one has taken the trouble to elaborate on the laws of relations. Is it not by chance that the *regulars* would have their head raised with their *regularity*? And would they not be similar to that man who, arriving late to a large gathering, succeeded in placing himself at the first rank by turning the world upside-down and crying to those who wished to imitate him: "You may not."

Such is done, or wishes to be done, by those who consider themselves as regulars; they do not try to help anyone, but make all their efforts to impede the works of those who, with good faith and good will, march in advance with their eyes fixed on the ideal.

Villarino del Villar.

ENDNOTES

1. Let us cite, among the other Rose-Croix who contributed to the new creation: J.-T. Desaguliers, James Anderson, G. Payne, King, Clavat, Lumden, Madden, Elliot.
2. *Traité méthodique de Science occulte,* on the legend of Hiram.
3. *Satan Démasqué.*
4. From l'Aulnaye, *Thuileur général,* p. 58 (note).
5. *Doctrine du Mal.*
6. The readers who wish to study the symbols on serious bases are invited to acquaint themselves with a very beautiful work of *M. Emile Soldi-Colbert de Beaulieu* on THE SACRED LANGUAGE. This is one of the rare contemporary authors who has seen clearly in the chaos of symbolism.
7. In our opinion, the black indicates above all passage from one plane to another, resurrection across death. From there, that consecration to Christ and to the symbolic Hiram.
8. *Thuileur,* p. 73 (note).
9. *Thuileur,* p. 89 (note).
10. Ragon, *Orthodoxie maconnique,* p. 29.
11. *Théosophes et franc-macons* (no. 5 of Lotus).
12. Ragon, *Orthodoxie maconnique,* p. 101.
13. See Fabre d'Olivet, *De l'etat social de l'homme,* Saint-Yves d'Alveyred, *Mission des Juifs;* Simon, *la Cité chinoise.*
14. Eliphas Lévi, *Histoire de la Magie,* p. 399 and foll.
15. Ragon, *loc. cit.*
16. Lenoir, *la Franc-Maconnerie,* pl 287.
17. *Thuileur des trent-trois degrés de l'Éclssisme du rite ancien, dit accepté,* p. 244.
18. Clavel, *Histoire pittoresque de la Franc-Maçonnerie,* p. 54.
19. See in the *Revue Hiram* (6 Rue de Savoie) the article by Teder on this symbolism.
20. Formula of recognition in the degree of Master.